Down (But Not Out) in Beijing and Shanghai –

The Comedy Side of Business in China

Kelsey Cole

 New Generation **Publishing**

Introduction

I've been travelling to, working in, and living in China for the past 13 years. I can honestly say there are very few experiences left in life to match the extreme swings in emotion, incredulity and amazement I've had during that time.

I always say to first-timers, China is a country you will either love or hate. There is no in-between. A good friend put it well, "Visit China for a week and you can write a book, stay there for a month and you can't write a postcard." This is one of the most accurate observations I've heard, along with my wife's summation after spending ten days there on holiday back in 2009. As we boarded the plane to go home I asked her to sum up the country. She did so in two words: "Fantastically disgusting". A truer evaluation I have still not heard, yet every time I go back she says she is envious of me.

One of my other favourites is that China is the '100-foot country'. Everything from 100 feet away looks wonderful, but the closer you get the more you see the cracks and imperfections become apparent. This is true if you consider almost any aspect of China, from a physical building to the way that business works and performs.

From the moment the plane door opens on your arrival in one of the major airports, China is fully in your face. The experience of the SARS outbreak when immigration people immediately invaded the plane in full chemical gear, to "the smell", you know you have arrived and you get your first taste of what is to come. In fairness there are some good things compared to the bad points of many global hub airports. When you arrive in China you are normally faced with multiple immigration desks... and people actually manning them.

Getting into China is honestly a very simple thing to achieve once you have that visa. There are many different expectations and realities for people visiting China for the first time. I remember my first trip to China in 2000, going in on a tourist visa. I mention this as, prior to going to China for the first time, I had been travelling around the world extensively, but because I was on a tourist visa and I knew literally nothing about China, I didn't take my laptop, cell phone or anything associated with working. Completely naive maybe, but don't forget this is a communist country, and it can be brutal.

You may remember the recent case of the dairy that watered down its baby milk with melamine. That incident killed many babies and hospitalised thousands more. This is the type of reality check you can experience: China is not a country focused on ethics and morals. Make sure when you get on that plane, wherever you are travelling from, to detach those elements from your psyche. Failure to do so may result in you being an emotional wreck, not just during your time there, but for a long time after. That is not saying what happens is right or wrong and it is not my intention to give anyone a lecture on ethics and morals, but culture is something we all think we know about, yet very few people really do understand or appreciate it. Culture for me is not about right or wrong, it's about differences and being able to understand those differences. I will not preach about 'my culture this', or 'my culture that', what I believe is essential is to understand the different global cultures and learn from the best parts in all of them.

Taking your understanding from a television programme like *Idiot Abroad*, broadcast in the UK, gives a really good insight into how the majority of people lack appreciation of other cultures. Add to this that the current so-called 'global superpower' has a population where fewer than 10% of people have a passport, and most get their news from local broadcasters who in reality have no interest in what happens outside the USA. How well culturally aware are we, really? More Europeans tend to travel, mainly backpacking when they are young, normally with the aim of drinking all the bars in some remote Asian location dry. Or to the Costas where people practise their language capabilities – specifically the British who, when the server does not speak "perfect English", just shout a bit louder.

Fundamentally to understand culture you have to experience day-to-day life for an extended duration. A week's holiday tells you a place is hot, the beer is cheap and you have a new mate called Miguel who is a taxi driver. Live and work there for six months (minimum) and the realities of life really start to come home. Consider how many people leave to live in another country for the 'new lifestyle', yet within a year are back in their originating country as they miss something you can never, nor should you as this has to be one of the reasons for moving there, recreate elsewhere. Culture is so important.

So back to China culture. It is hugely varied as you would expect, however the 'normal' people are generally very friendly and intrigued by other cultures and nations. At the same time Chinese people are very nationalistic and negative comments about China will never go down well. Understanding the cultural norms is a real must before you get on that plane. For example, leaving food on your plate is an important gesture as it shows you have been given enough. In the West we often take this to mean the food was crap! It is important to understand that China has been, and continues to be, a country with huge issues feeding its population, hence the cultural differences with something as simple as eating. Another very simple but dramatic difference between western and Chinese cultures is the minute you walk off the plane you will see people spitting. It normally draws groans of disgust from the virgin visitors and even some of the regulars – who have never got used to it – however the biggest insult when eating in China is to put your hand to your mouth and remove a piece of food. Their norm is to spit it out. Two simple, but very immediate cultural differences to consider when going to China.

There are other cultural differences, specifically when it comes to doing business. In China the local practice is to get the Lao Wa (foreigner) off balance by starting meetings late, pushing to finish early and in between making sure the meeting rooms are cold in winter and hot in summer. These tactics are common and it is vital you prepare for them.

When asked how long you have got for a meeting, make sure the people you are meeting with understand, 'as long as it takes'. Otherwise the meeting will start, and then it is followed swiftly by a lunch with many *campei* (bottoms up) drinking rice wine (sub note: this one of the major reasons I packed up drinking alcohol). Lunch is like being in France, ie very extended, then it's back to the office and, oh, before you know, it's time to leave for dinner (another sub note: dinner starts early in China around 17:30). The evening will continue with a trip to the KYTV club or some such other place where everyone will pretend to be your friend. At least, the replacement B Team will be there for that, now that you are wrecked and their A Team having left and been in bed for 4 hours already. You finally finish at about 01:30.

It is important to recognise these business tactics and, whether you are a drinker or not, be assured to this day these tactics are still employed with relish. Drinking a Chinese person under the table may be seen as a victory for the visiting Westerner, but don't be fooled by the fact they will have watered down their drinks and they will be *campeiing* you in rotation.

One tip I would strongly recommend, if indeed you want to go down this route, and that is to play your hosts at their own game and have your own bottle of "rice wine", which is really water, and substitute it. Trust me you will need to do this. On my very first trip I fell foul of the tactics, and at 03:00 hit the sack and was woken up on a Saturday morning at 07:00 to be told, "We go to work." I had the mother of all headaches and felt like I had been in the boxing ring with Mike Tyson for 12 rounds... a real ugly feeling!

Just to finish off this specific trip, after work I was taken to a famous lake in Nanjing where, if I had one dollar for every person who wanted a photograph of me with someone, I could have retired. In those days it was rare to see a Lao Wa in such places, and one with no hair on their head, but hair on their arms was considered a real freak show! So having played the freak for an hour or so, I was dumped at the bus station with a Taiwanese guy who was heading back to Shanghai. I need to point out this journey would take approximately four hours by bus, something my still fragile state was not particularly looking forwards to. I got on the bus and had settled down in my seat to watch the Chinese TV with English subtitles, when a lady tried to get on with a small dog. Not speaking a word of Chinese wasn't an issue in this situation. The driver was not happy and they had a bit of a shouting match, after which the lady left the bus crying.

Okay, so the drama was over... or so I thought.

7

Next thing her 'partner' gets on the bus and drags the bus driver out and then promptly the two of them have a Jackie Chan and Bruce Lee kick off in the bus station! Within a minute they were surrounded by a crowd and money started changing hands... people were betting on the outcome. It was at this point it dawned on me that my guy, who was clearly Jackie Chan, was going to get his back side kicked by Bruce Lee. Not good news as it was going to be difficult to get back to Shanghai if the bus driver ended up heading to a hospital in the back of an ambulance. Action was needed. Despite the protestations of my Taiwanese tour guide, I got off the bus broke into the ring and dragged my driver by the coat collar back onto the bus. I think he was pretty relieved and slammed the door shut before Bruce Lee could get on. Off we set minus a lady and a dog.

Another heads up about in relation to travelling. When you are told it's 'about an hour' to a destination, by car, it is at least double that and additionally most drivers over there have no idea where they are going. Satnav is still very new and on top of this new roads are appearing on a daily basis. One recommendation is that you plan your "natural" or "comfort" breaks around this. Whilst it may be normal for local people to relieve themselves at a convenient point – for themselves – it is something many Westerners may not be too comfortable with. My suggestion.....have one less cup of coffee or tea before you set off for your journey into the unknown

Flights historically have been pretty good in terms of departure and arrival times, however travelling out of Shanghai, Beijing or Hong Kong nowadays, you must expect a one to three hour delay, normally with you sitting on the place. Inconvenient for internal or local flights, however a bit more challenging if you are flying intercontinental and have 12 to 14 hours of flying ahead of you…..

Be wary of taxi drivers. They have an innate greed for money and as you generally have no idea where you are or where you are going they will as standard take you the long way around anywhere. A sub note here for your is there have been increasing cases of registered taxis putting electric motors into the odometers to speed them up so passengers get charged for a further distance that they have travelled. Be warned, going back to Shanghai PuDong airport is a treasure trove for these corrupt drivers. Make sure you have change and not just big notes. They will take your bags out first. You hand over the large denomination notes and as you get your bags together they jump back into the taxi and take off with the doors open, leaving you with no change and no *fapiao* (receipt). 80% of people I have spoken to have openly admitted this has happened to them at that airport.

Whilst China is generally a very safe place to be for the Lao Wa it is also very important to understand in their eyes you are there to be removed of your cash. You are seen as real live ATM, but recognise this and prepare for the challenges. Chinese people generally do not like conflict and Lao Wa tend to be more protected as the state does not like bad publicity if something happens to them.

If you do venture into clubs and bars, they are generally the worst places to be fleeced. There are local expectations if someone is talking to you they will ask for a drink. They will have some type of coloured water and for the privilege you will end up with a $50.00 bill. It is very easy to run up a four figure bill on a Saturday night (or any night for that matter), and when you question the bill things can get a little uncomfortable…..you figure it out

Another group to be wary of is road users. The automotive industry in China is at best 13 years old (at the time of writing). 20 years ago there were two taxis in the whole of Shanghai. Today there are approximately 16,000 which sounds huge except the population is 24,000,000. When it rains you can *never* get a taxi! Back in 2000 the only cars on the road were taxis, government cars and Buick vans. Today in the region of 25,000 new cars a month are arriving on the roads in Shanghai alone. The vast majority of those new cars are being driven by first time drivers, and a huge number of these people may never have driven a car before their 'driving test'.

However I digress so back to the taxis…..If you show a taxi driver a locator card, some of the magnifying glasses they get out of their glove boxes would actually allow you to see the insides of the craters on the moon. Another point is that many of the taxi drivers are also not from the city you are in and therefore they are probably as lost as you are. Don't get excited if they wind down the window to ask someone else for directions….. frequently. Another category is drivers employed by companies. One particular Mad Max, who I always requested, was a guy with a real interesting history. He was a driver in the last Chinese war and was the only survivor of his platoon. The distance from JiangYin to Shanghai is approximately 170 km and he would complete this trip door to door in 1 hour 15 minutes, where other drivers would take closer to 3 hours. He drove like every day was his last, but the positive is he seemed to have luck on his side.

Driving schools are a concept that have been heard of and do exist, but beware of the Shanghai Volkswagen Santana's with a black and white chequered pattern. Invariably there are five or six people in the car, the 'instructor' in the front passenger seat, chain smoking and grabbing the wheel occasionally to steer the vehicle away from some poor unsuspecting pedestrian on a main road. Many of these cars have bald or cracked tyres, some have one wing mirror (never two) and plastic-covered, blacked-out windows – which you can't see into, nor can you see out of. Usually these are the front and rear side passenger windows and occasionally the rear one. In fairness the only part of a vehicle that *has* to function is the horn, and much like in India, it's there for guidance to let other drivers know 'I'm here'!

The good thing is that all new cars are issued without a licence plate and these generally take a month to arrive. Therefore it's easy to spot new drivers and find ways to avoid them. This, however, can also be used to the advantage of the less scrupulous. A very good friend of mine, from the Netherlands, who was an ex-pat living in Shanghai and who was a little challenged to get up early in a morning, would occasionally perform the following... Leaving his apartment later than he should the first thing he would do is remove the licence plates from his car and put them in the trunk. He would them drive like the locals – ie a lunatic, at about warp factor 1 – and laugh out loud as the flashes went off on every speed camera photographing the space where his licence plates should be. Arriving at a convenient Starbucks close to his destination, I would go get the drinks whilst he screwed the licence plates back on...

As a small note on the new drivers, a very good Chinese friend of mine went to take his driving test in 2010. Before he went for his test he had actually never driven a car. He was stunned when he failed his test. The story does however have a 'happy' ending: a week later he re-sat his test and passed. Again you have been warned.

There does seem to be some sort of hierarchy relating to vehicles and there are certain licence plates that if seen all vehicles have to get out of their way…even the police, Passenger buses seem to command the road, trucks tend to hog the road and passenger cars drive wherever there is a road… correct side or not. One fun game to play at night is spot-the-vehicle. People riding electric scooters, for example, have this belief it's better if you ride without lights as it saves the battery life….shame it doesn't save the owners life. Bikes and scooters are not the only ones following this policy. Cars, buses and trucks all seem to think it is others who should have their lights on and there is no reason for them to light up…..except the next cigarette.

It's always fun when a Chinese Sebastian Vettel drives slalom style down a motorway at night with only the rev counter to guess the speed, as the odometer stopped working two days out of the car showroom and cannot be fixed. The real fun is spotting the truck doing 15 kilometres per hour in the outside lane with no lights on, when a Mad Max impersonator is doing 180 kilometres per hours and is actually clinically blind. You think I joke.

This introduction was designed to give you a small, but general, flavour of some aspects of the Chinese way of life, but the main reason for this tome is to share with you the realities of doing business in China based on real experiences with real people and real companies.

Separately to this book, I have for a number of year's written blogs on my travels, more as a way of explaining myself to my daughter when she is old enough to appreciate why I've rarely been at home during her formative years. One of these blogs I shared with my sister-in-law, a beautiful lady who has never been on an aeroplane, never stayed in a hotel and only been outside the UK once (on a day trip). She read my blog and came back to me saying, "It made me cry, it made me laugh, I could not stop reading... I didn't know you could write fiction." To which my response was very simple, "Sweetheart, it's all based on fact". She still does not believe me to this day.

To the old hands of Chinese business who read this you know exactly what I am talking about. To those of you who have visited for a week or two, have received the 'royal' treatment, and now see themselves as experts on China, you are some of the most naive people living on the planet. Your blind faith in a local management who tell you "China is different....." Believing them above the ex-patriots who are living and dealing with the consequences on a daily basis yet at the same time are trying to implement your company culture, and then you remove them as the local management team sees them as a nuisance and not understanding China or how it works. The only people that can give you a chance of redemption.........the same people that were the leaders in their fields before they were despatched off to China...... Considering your MBAs, PHDs and other salubrious TLAs (Three Letter Acronyms) you want to stick after your names, do yourself a favour a take your heads from up your arses and understand the realities of life, not just your very cosy and safe corporate-world headquarters.

Considering the intelligence of people that make it to be 'captains of industry', it is truly staggering how little they know about the world outside their corporate spread sheets. For those sitting in those roles and reading this, you may not like what you read in this section, but ignore it at your peril. If you did any analysis on joint ventures in China it would look an awful lot like the statistics for marriage in many western countries today, only worse. Even setting up your own wholly-owned foreign entity (WOFE) is plagued with risk if you do not resource it correctly. For you corporate types this means making sure your company culture is instilled from Day 1, and for you finance experts out there it involves an awful lot of costs for the services of capable expatriates. Back to the analogy of marriage and joint ventures. Marriage, to work, is something that is based on mutual and in most cases implicit trust. It's exactly the same in a joint venture. If your partner has had six previous "relationships", its normally a good sign that they can't stay faithful…but sometimes love – or in the case of a joint venture the promise of huge profits – makes people blind……

One final comment to those of the corporate world, who think this is complete rubbish, and they are for sure correct let me ask a question. When you started up your new business / facility / operation in Mexico or Central Europe, or even in your home country, did you say, as you sat in your cosy offices with plush carpets, manicured PAs and wall-to-wall Starbucks coffee machines, "Let's leave this to the locals to set up. I'm sure our company culture will happen as a matter of fact." You all know the answer to that. There were bus-loads of willing and non-willing victims despatched over to the new location for weeks and months on end to ensure the systems were put in place, to make sure the company logo was on the building just perfectly, to make sure that walking in it looked just like your 'flagship' facility in Detroit, Paris or where ever. The corporate work wear was immaculate and all those little things like 'health and safety' actually mattered… oh and you had instilled LEAN and Kaizen Teams, etc. Get the message yet? No? Well why did you do it in those countries and not in South East Asia where it was needed more than anywhere? Well the answer is clearly contained in this section however fundamentally it's due to a huge dollop of cultural ignorance and distance. It's not a short flight across one of your international borders, you actually need something more than a passport or ID card to get there….you will actually need a visa, hardly a complicated thing to get. I wonder how many of those "captains of industry" spend multiple weekends away from home in some remote part of the world ensuring their future operation is going to be a success in essence getting their hands dirty? From experience it is the "vast minority" as it might interfere with their private lives or other gigs they have got going, and besides which there are other people to make this stuff happen….right!!!

A Lessons Learnt Programme

This Lessons Learnt Programme was executed for an automotive manufacturing company to look back on situations resulting from a major acquisition programme, with specific focus on one facility in Shanghai. This facility was one of five sold to the new company from Shenzhen, Chongqing and Shanghai as part of the company buy out which resulted in the company trebling in size.

At this point I feel I should be adding a disclaimer as they do on some TV shows: "The names and characters in this book have been changed to protect the innocent". Although in reality with this case the names have been changed to protect the guilty.

Things go wrong because of people. "People" - in these circumstances fall into three categories:

1) Some will allow things to happen that shouldn't
2) Some will encourage things that shouldn't be allowed to happen
3) Others will try to address the issues that shouldn't be happening

For those in the first section it generally comes down to a lack of knowledge, experience and being in the wrong job. For the second group, they are the ones who have two Sunseeker yachts in exotic locations, bank accounts in countries that most people have never heard of, and a range of other assets that their meagre salary could never substantiate. The third section is a small, dedicated band of people who for some strange reason actually believe that doing things the right way makes sense.

The acquisition company had a facility in China

prior to the acquisition that employed some 150 people. The company being purchased had over 2,000 people in five facilities. Due diligence was not done correctly, and could not have been, as there were only two people in China from the acquisition company that were capable of performing due diligence. The acquisition company had, as a point of note, a Wholly Owned Foreign Entity (WOFE) and was being run by Western expatriates at the time of acquiring.

The company being acquired was, simply put, completely the opposite of the purchasing company. There was one expatriate who was considered to be always crying wolf in Corporate, complaining about the corruption and asking for help to deal with it. The operations in China had been set up by someone we shall call 'The Fixer'. The Fixer is someone most companies from the West employ in China and it is pretty easy to identify them. Generally this is someone who speaks relatively good English, has probably been educated, at some time, outside China and comes across well to the corporate seagulls. They will quickly pick up on corporate buzzwords, tell people that they know everyone and add in a mix of corporate legal stuff they Google'd on the internet. Before long you have the Fixer in place helping you with everything, from where do you get toilet paper to organising your apartment, your kid's induction at the private international schools, to how the joint ventures are physically set up and who's running them.

The particular Fixer from the company in question was the son of a Chinese military attaché to the embassy in Moscow. He was an American Chinese or Chinese American (actually this depended on which country he was in at the time). He clearly had a warped sense of humour to be fair as he claimed to also be a part time lecturer in business ethics at a very well-known American university. He also managed to pay – in cash – $1,000,000 to buy an apartment in one of the swanky areas in Shanghai overlooking the Jin Mao tower, after only seven years as Mr Fixer! His official corporate pay cheque did not support such a lifestyle…....

In addition to Mr Fixer there were other key players, the most significant of those was the person we shall refer to as the 'Head Snake'. The Head Snake was the owner of the private joint-venture partner the company being bought was in bed with. These individuals created the platform and process to allow the money to flow in the right directions…..ie their bank accounts. It is important to point out, at this stage, all the operations in China of the company being acquired were joint ventures with three different private joint-venture partners, all set up by Mr Fixer.

This process covered a two year period in the late 2000s, and as a point of note the last time I heard the acquisition company still had in excess of 30 western expatriates now living and working in China, on minimum 24 month contracts. I think they did learn the lessons, but in fairness the only reason was that one of their senior executives actually lived in China and was able to paint a picture the rest of the board was forced to accept – albeit they could not believe what was happening or what they were hearing. The results, however, did finally focus their minds…

General

The significance of the cultural differences between the West and China are very badly misunderstood by the majority of Westerners.

I have already detailed some of the more simple and obvious differences and misunderstandings, however adapting to these differences is a significant challenge. The adaptation to different cultures, and then finding a way to work effectively, is very draining both mentally and physically. A good example of this is a simple hotel contract. Your company has a contract with a hotel (can be a local brand or for that matter a very famous international one). You arrive at the hotel and are advised there are no "standard rooms" available and they are trying to upgrade you to a more expensive room. You go through a twenty minute routine, talking with the check in personnel....who then gets a supervisor.....who then gets the Manager. During this time you have to get your laptop out and pull up a copy of the signed contract showing the fixed rate pricing and agreement that if the hotel is full then you are upgraded to a higher class of room at the cost of a standard room. Then you are advised the internet will cost such-and-such amount per day, so again you point to the contract... then laundry charges... so you again point out the contract. Three weeks later going back to the same hotel it's *deja vu*. This is a stereotypical format of the daily "fighting" that is gone through in a work environment also. It's not just one element or area (ie just work or hotels) it's really across the full range of your daily life. Dealing with taxi drivers, going shopping in the 'supermarkets' etc...

− Joint-venture partners often believe they have the

same perceived common goal, but frequently in reality each of the two parties hold a different idea of what the goal is.

Your company's goal of taking over significant market share and building a strong base to support your global OEMs is not what your average Mr Fixer is interested in. Their interest is in how much cash you are going to put down, so they can see how much they can get out. Assuming you are going to make a lot of money quickly is not a realistic goal. Ensuring you have a very clear and defined strategy is vital. Before you sign on the dotted line talk to as many different companies and people who have been in, or are in, such relationships. Knowledge in these situations really is power.

- Joint venture companies in China can work, BUT they have to be managed, run and controlled by westerners and have a strong western company management team in place, ensuring the company work ethic and mind set are instilled from day one. Can you transition to a local management Team, absolutely. It all depends on how you go about the process and ensure the Team you are building is "indoctrinated" in your company culture in your "best in class" facilities and regions and colleagues. Timing to achieve this will fully depend on if you have identified the right local managers and their ability to adapt and learn to manage. Don't think a two week induction programme will suffice, it absolutely won't.

Talk to any expatriate currently, or historically, living in China and within 15 minutes they'll be saying, "...been there, done that..." Their experiences are very similar, no matter the industry they are involved in. The root cause of all their frustrations will invariably be the lack of understanding and support of the challenges and issues of doing business in China from the corporate managers sitting in 'fantasia land'.

As mentioned in the introduction, unfortunately there is a general perception from the Western management teams that expatriates tend to be negative, and belief in the local personnel is unquestionable. Consider here why this may be the case. Most people in the West will speak one language fluently and in other cases, due to the fact the English is still considered the "International" language. Large companies will have a number of people speaking common languages like French, German, Spanish and Italian. How many people in those companies speak fluent Mandarin? The vast majority of people going to China for the first time will unfortunately lower their guard once someone starts to speak to the in English (the common business language over there), and the first thing you do subconsciously is trust them.

- Spoken English was exceptionally poor in all levels of the Shanghai business. The ability to effectively communicate at all levels of the business has as a result been severely challenged. The message has frequently not got through – either accidentally or deliberately.

Written English is normally pretty good, but even then the meaning of an email and lack of ownership that results causes more issues than it fixes.

- Never underestimate the 'brain washing' of the majority of Chinese people. Blood is thicker than water. Westerners can be seen as 'evil' manipulators. This is another element of culture and the only relief for a Westerner is that the Japanese are hated even more. Go back to the recent unrest in China and the destruction of anything Japanese – cars, TVs etc. This sentiment goes back to the atrocities from the Second World War. This dislike fully unites all Chinese people, despite the roots of it being many, many years ago. A strong recommendation is to read and understand something about the historical conflicts in South East Asia. During the Presidential elections in Taiwan some years back the Chinese fired a missile that landed close to Taiwan, just to make sure then remembered who really they answer to.

- Once an acquisition is made, immediately after the deal is closed install a full western team to implement your own company's best practices and run the company. This is especially true for the IT systems. Do not sit back and accept the fact the Enterprise Resource Planning (ERP) system has to be in Mandarin, even if the cost for change is a significant amount.

The point here is that in China ERP systems are seen as unnecessary. The majority of suppliers will have one, maybe two, customers and therefore as the customer you have a significant hold over them. This again leads to some very poor practices, and suppliers who honestly should not be in business doing some absurd business practices. Additionally without an ERP system in use your ability to control not just materials, but the suppliers used is somewhere between zero and none. An example of this was a situation where on an inter-company purchase a mandated instruction was given to source a specific product. Speaking to the GM of the inter-company supplier a month later he told me he had never received any additional orders. On checking with the material controller he, individually, chose which supplier to buy this product from, and this could change on a delivery by delivery basis. Don't be fooled into thinking this was done for the benefit of the business, it was simply which supplier gave him the biggest hongbao (bribe) for that shipment.

Another point to note that due to the endemic lack of system use it is generally very challenging to change any system. Taking a corrupt cog out of a manual system will result in the whole system crashing at a very rapid speed, as that cog will be the only one that can execute that specific task. Secondly if you instil your own ERP system you have the ability to host it in your home country and manage the data integrity. Bills of materials are the fibres that hold the supply chain together, but they can and will be manipulated to create supply issues, if you believe a local ERP Team will implement. Anything that is seen as taking a responsibility off someone who is making money from it does not go down well with the locals.

- During the due diligence process ensure you get a complete list of every person signed up to the confidentiality agreement on the programme. Talk to as many of them as possible – not just the people designated to make the sale.

Remember the people put in front of you will have a vested interest in selling the business. Their bonuses will rely on making sure you pay top dollar for a pup. Take the time to talk to the people who are actually doing the work, then you have a chance of uncovering the truth, not what people think you want to hear.

- In cases of buying a company involved with joint ventures, ensure the history of the joint-venture partner is thoroughly investigated, and where possible talk to previous western partners of that JV.

The joint-venture partner for this facility is currently on their eighth willing victim today. Yet another company from the West that thinks all the other companies they had JVs with just got it completely wrong, and they will be able to make everything right. Oh, as a side note it is their first time experience of manufacturing in China..... Probably some potential consultation opportunities coming up.... ☺

- Traceability in the Shanghai operation was virtually non-existent. All processes and activities appeared to have been verbal and were only carried in the heads of certain individuals. This comment also relates back to the point about IT systems. Whilst the company had an ERP system, it was only there to act as a follow up to the manual processes.

Observing the way things work in China would make most LEAN (is a production practice that considers the expenditure of resources for any goal other than the creation of value for the end customer to be wasteful, and thus a target for elimination) people run to the nearest shrink. But remember there are lots of people in China and the government want as many of them working as possible, so where in the West you will automate as much of the manual work as possible, this is absolutely the opposite in China. The other reason this is relevant is that the standard practices of work are fully open to being corrupted, and no matter what piece of paper you get signed to protect your company's moral position it is not worth the paper it is written on in China, the law will always support the locals.

Another factor concerning traceability was lack of local network drive. All information would be saved on individuals laptops or desktops and more frequently than would be admitted that information would just disappear. In the case of design information, this would normally be leaked to a competitor. One evening I happened to be at a restaurant having dinner with a friend when I spotted our 'loan' American Chinese Engineer passing documents over to a friend at dinner on another table. This individual, because of where we were sitting, did not see us. The next day he reported that his designs for a specific product for a specific customer had been stolen from his laptop. When questioned by the western President the 'loan' Engineer denied ever being in the restaurant. The "friend" he was meeting used to be the Engineering Director at the company, and was now working for a direct competitor of ours.

-   The automotive industry in China is very immature and therefore experienced personnel in the industry will not be found easily. You will need to spend time, money and personal effort to train up the local team to get them to the levels you expect. They do not come ready made. Inside the company it was confirmed that 'Someone', 'No One' and 'It's Not My Fault' were the three most common surnames. There is a huge difference culturally in the way people work between the West and countries like China. Giving a local employee in that situation responsibility to think and act for themselves was pure madness

–   Young Chinese business people believe they have a given right to huge compensation packages to do nothing. An example of this was the hiring of a HR Director from the local market place who came with a six-figure US$ salary and package. He exited within three months. The individual knew nothing, but managed to persuade his next victim company he was worth more and off he went.

– Nepotism is a word that was created in China.

The Head Snake basically controlled the supply chain. One brother-in-law owned the moulding supplier, his sister owned a stamping shop. Another relative owned the rubber moulding supplier and his children and their husbands were either responsible for the sales or purchasing of the joint-venture companies.

– Expectations in Europe and the Americas of the skill level of local Chinese personnel are too high and totally unrealistic. It is not a lack of schooling, or the fact that everyone seems to have or be studying for an MBA etc. The education system is China is very good, and there are a lot of very intelligent Chinese people. However, if you got one dollar for every time you heard at the end of a phone on a conference call from Europe or North America, "Why can't you get the data from that guy? … It's not acceptable … get that data from him … we can get that data everywhere else" most old hands could have retired to a personal island paid for in cash.

It gets to a point, and I used this tactic personally on a number of occasions by saying 'TIC.' There would be a stunned silence on the call before saying, "This Is China!" Even people visiting for a week who saw the attitudes and behaviour at first hand, would, within a week of returning, to the motherland be making calls and saying, "Why can't you get the data from that guy? … It's not acceptable … get that data from him … we can get that data everywhere else." Many years ago I was asked by a CEO, "What is the definition of insanity…" I replied "I am not sure Sir". To which he replied, "Doing the same thing, the same way, and expecting different results". Sometimes it was a question you would ask yourself about the Corporate seagulls……..

– Always have an exit strategy prepared. The first step in considering a joint venture in China has to be your exit strategy. How do you get out if, no when, it goes wrong? Don't let the gloss of having a new far-flung facility in your empire overrun your business instincts.

– Understanding from Europe or the Americas as to what was going on did not exist. They did not believe what they were being told. 'TIC!' ☺

– There is no substitute for real time experience. Spending a few days in China, even a few weeks, gives only the smallest glimpses of reality. Living, breathing and working in the environment for 6 months (as a minimum) is the only way westerners will be able to start to influence and effect change. Believing you can be successful in China without instilling your own business culture and that has to start with a western management team is redefining insanity.

Before going to China, breathing and air quality is something that people suffering any form of asthma may want to seriously consider. One of the main developments over the past 13 years has been the worsening of the air pollution. A good friend of mine living out there had to go for an annual medical to check the levels of mercury in him. The smog is so bad there are literally a handful of days in a year when it's worth going up one of the main towers in Shanghai to get a panoramic view of the city. It's truly pot luck and guesswork when those days will arrive.

– The bench strength of the company acquiring the business was not strong enough to take over a business in crisis

Whilst the WOFE employees were well disciplined and well trained they had no experience to deal with the challenges of the company they were purchasing. The local management team believed that they could manage the company from afar, however when they did get involved and spend time there they quickly followed the same poor practices that had plagued the company up to that point

– Implementation of the New Product Introduction (NPI) process was deliberately not supported by the local management team. Pleading non-understanding of the training was completely out of order, and set the business back by at least 12 months. This continued to allow projects to be managed in a totally unstructured way, resulting in multiple visit to customers apologising and assuring it would not happen again … and then having to repeat the exercise the following week.

– Taking snakes out of the business was a clear priority, but the implications are not immediately visible, they were the ones generally who knew how the systems operated.

– Snakes were prevalent at all levels, and in all functions, of the Shanghai business.

I was asked to sit with our VP of Asia and explain to him the activity I had been working on at one of our smaller joint-venture companies. As I explained the details and situation you could visibly see the colour draining from his face. During this conversation my colleague crept up to the door in boardroom and yanked it open. The Chinese Sales Manager fell into the room, he had been listening at the door during the entire conversation. He a month later, he turned up as the Sales Manager of the plastic moulding company controlled by the Head Snake.

We also found out that the offices of the Lao Wa had been bugged. It took some time to uncover. however, if we were going to discuss something specifically confidential it was always done off site in a neutral location like a hotel lobby.

– The Purchasing Manager at the Wuxi facility believed the business could turn the Asia Purchasing Director – one of the sons-in-law of the Head Snake – into a 'good guy'. At best naive, at worst it showed his lack of desire and ability to get involved with fixing the deep routed and fundamental issues.

This specific son-in-law was caught red handed in a, shall we say, a less than professional and ethical way. He was fired and then promptly decided to sue for compensation. The case went to court. During the court case that lasted approximately three months, the fired individual's legal team claimed there was a document their client had never received from the company. His legal team during the trial recognised that if this document had existed it would stand their client in a much better condition for success. Mysteriously towards the end of the case, they produced the said document with an official company 'chop', despite having repeated multiple times it did not exist. For those not familiar with a 'chop' it's basically a rubber stamp with the company details embossed on it. In China is used as a signature for any official purpose, ie it replaces a person's signature. Now as you might appreciate it is pretty easy to copy a rubber stamp. It was not one of our official 'chops' as they were kept closely guarded under lock and key. So when in court we were able to prove to the judge that the letter had actually been printed on his legal team's office printer and the chop was not genuine, the judge told the sacked person's legal team, "You should not have fabricated this letter," We thought this excellent news and meant the judge was sure to throw the case out. Err... no, he awarded the case to the fired employee. TIC!

− Up until February 2009, employees who has access to the local ERP system and had left the company still had access directly into email and the ERP systems.

In some cases these people had left the company more than 12 months previously and had been working for the snakes at other companies, with direct access to bills of materials, pricing from suppliers, customer pricing etc.

− There were no network or backup drives for data to be stored. This resulted in all information being stored on individual PCs, and generally being deleted when employees left the company.

When the Projects Manager left his laptop was confiscated and analysed. Not only was there huge amounts of sensitive information he should never have had access to on it, also significant amounts of material that were only stored on his machine. Maybe what he was really concerned about was the vast array of pictures and videos on there that had absolutely nothing to do with any products we manufactured.......

− There was a genuine feeling of fear in the business

in December 2008 due to the reach of the head snakes.

This was and remains a serious issue when working in such companies. The structure in a Chinese company can be viewed as being very similar to traditional German companies. The person who runs the company makes all the decisions and nothing happens unless they give the order. With the local family being in all the high positions it was a real fear felt by the employees, and in some cases they have disappeared. What happened to them you will never know. One day they are working in the company and the next day no one even remembers their name.

Prior to the sacking of the Asia Purchasing Director, I started digging into the files and archives for evidence. I asked one of the buyers in the office (who must have learnt his English from Trevor Peacock of *Vicar of Dibley* fame) to help me find some information. I have never seen such pure fear in a person in my life. He was shaking like he was having a fit. I found out later he had been ordered not to help the Lao Wa by the said Purchasing Director. He genuinely felt threatened and I can only imagine what that specific details of the threat were.

– Destruction of incriminating documentation by snakes happens.

A large number of files were removed from store rooms, specifically things like human resources records, financial data and purchase orders. At one point we held a truce meeting with the Head Snake where we agreed not to prosecute on certain aspects provided the records were returned. The records, which had been "lost", came back allowing us to close out a local government requirement.

– Forgery of documentation by snakes.

This was and remained a serious issue in all levels of the company. The fundamental integrity you have with a customer is in the Production Part Approval Process (PPAP) submission. It is the documentation you submit with your parts telling the customer their status. These were regularly fabricated. Copy and paste technology was widely used. Simply put, this is just lying to your customer and has huge potential implications.

– Cutting corners was a practice discovered by the Head Snake and honed to perfection in the Shanghai facility.

This is something you will find in general in China. If we talk about the Advanced Product Quality Planning (APQP) process it is there for a reason. It basically guides you though a consistent process to ensure you can consistently deliver programmes in line with your processes and the customers' needs. By-passing this is like saying "when I get up in the morning I am going to put my jacket on and forgetting all about my shirt". Why would you want to do that? Well the simple reason is that, unlike getting dressed, a project is not something that generally starts and finishes in a very short period of time, so in essence the mind-set is, "I don't know why I need to do this and it does not affect me, so I won't bother." Even if they do know why they need to do it they still do not do it, as it's "too much work."

– There was a lack of ownership across all parts of the Shanghai organisation. "It's not my job," could have been printed on everyone's jacket.

A serious point on this is that from birth the Chinese are literally brainwashed not to think for themselves. By doing this it makes life a lot easier to maintain control. Look at a simple analogy. India is supposed to be a democracy and there is, in all honesty, total chaos when it tries to control anything. China on the other hand is a communist country and is tightly controlled. To build a road in India will take ten to twenty years. To build the same road in China will take ten to twenty months, mainly due to poor planning they have to rip it up and re-lay it three times. How can the Chinese keep doing this? Simply by ordering people to do things. No questions will be asked and the job gets done. Was it right to do it? What are the implications of doing it? That may be thought about later, or most probably not at all. Don't get me wrong there are now more and more pressure groups growing in China and, despite the 100% control over the internet, there are still formats like Sina Webo. However there are lots of people who have voiced their concerns about freedom and are no longer 'free'. Again remember where you are. Put the focus on yourselves for a minute. Do you like people coming to where you live and telling you how you should live your lives?

Do not expect the majority of Chinese people to take initiative in a business process. Predominantly the Mr Fixers are the exception to this. Expecting otherwise is just redefining insanity.

A quality wall was installed at one point to ensure any non-conforming products arriving from the suppliers were identified and rejected on receipt. One week after installing this goods-inwards firewall, the Logistics personnel refused to carry on. Clearly it was impacting their financial gains…..!

– Strike letters, sent out by the Head Snake, were

found in the facility before, during and after a mass walk out in February 2009.

So what is wrong with that, you might ask? Well by this time the joint venture had ceased to exist. The Head Snake was no longer part of the business. He was already getting into bed with his next willing victim, yet he still had the power of fear in the employees. There were still snakes operating in the business and it took a long time to identify them all, in part due to the fear they created and the lack of willingness of others to come forwards and report them.

– Local management meetings could have been reduced in duration by 90% if the local management arrived when the meeting was scheduled and were focused on the meeting itself, not emails and phone calls.

Time management and meeting place discipline were totally lacking. Meetings were there to be seen at, not to be participated in. The majority of attendees would turn up with a small note book and a pen. "No one" would actually ever turn up with information ready to present. The 'managers' that had laptops came to the meetings and basically wrote and sent emails, or in some cases spent their time trawling the internet looking at things to buy with their new found wealth. One in particular must have by now equalled Imelda Marcos for shoes... and it was a he!

Another frustrating habit would be the answering of their telephones – the phones were never on mute, just blaring out some current "fashionable" ringtone at volume twenty – and then actually hold a conversation completely oblivious of anyone else in the room. A point of note here is that a Chinese person standing in

Shanghai can, I am sure, be heard by a person standing in Beijing… without the aid of a telephone. Speaking in anything less than a shout is something that is clearly not possible in China. I'm not sure if it's because they think the person they are talking to is a long way away, or they themselves are hard of hearing. If they are, then there are a lot of hard of hearing people in China.

One more to add to the list in this section is people wandering in and out of meetings. "Let's discuss this specific topic", was generally followed by someone going and making a call, waiting for another three people to turn up, a conversation to take place in Mandarin for five minutes and then the answer comes, "OK!!!" Err… *OK what, exactly*?

One good piece of advice for meetings in China is to make sure you ask the same question three different ways and see if you get a consistent answer. It's the best way to find out if they have understood anything you have said.

– Corporate seagulls should only be allowed into China if they have lived and worked there for a minimum of 12 months.

There is no substitute for living a situation on a daily basis to focus the mind on what has to be changed. Remote management in these situations will only allow the challenges to continue and become more serious and significant to your balance sheet. Should you decide to move any centralised function to China and not support it with the correct infrastructure will not show the bottom line results you were planning on, and will effectively cost you significantly more…..and probably more than a little hair loss

There was a Purchasing Council meeting in April 2008 in China. The participants travelled from the USA and Europe (agenda was Wuxi one and a half days, Shanghai one day) to 'fix China'. The meeting had to stop at 5pm in order for the attending Purchasing Directors to go visit the copy goods market!!! All meetings included the Head Snake's son-in-law, the Asia Purchasing Director. As a note prior to all the overseas attendees arriving I had briefed the Purchasing Leadership Team on the activities happening in Shanghai and the role of the Asia Purchasing Director. Despite this the Asia Purchasing Director was still invited, thus continuing to show a total lack of understanding of what was really going on. Even more shocking was the openness of confidential information shared whilst this person was in attendance…..of which I am confident none was shared with his father in law!!!!!!

– Blame culture was very prevalent in all areas of the business – internal and external.

The suppliers were easy targets and it destroyed a number of relationships. Just find another 'victim' instead of building a relationship. Responsibility is something the Chinese do not take seriously. There is no feeling of guilt, just embarrassment when they are caught doing something wrong.

– Effective sourcing in China requires significant technical support and changes of specifications (raw materials in Europe and the Americas are not readily available in China – they generally have to be imported).

There is a thriving copy resin market in Shanghai. Employees in companies who receive genuine overseas resins very carefully open the bags, empty the contents and then sell the empty bags. The bags are then re-filled and on-sold as genuine materials with all the original manufacturers' labels, bar codes, traceability details etc. What are they filled with… let's just say it won't be what you are expecting it to be.

An example here was a specific programme was calling up a grade of plastic resin that was not readily available in China. It was an imported grade from Europe. The Sales Director believing they knew more about this the Purchasing community decided the best way to source this material was to trawl the internet. A couple of hours later the triumphant Sales Director comes to the Purchasing office and tells the Asia Purchasing Director not only have they found the material in China, but it was going to be delivered the next day. In order to ensure this took place they had to pay cash in advance. It should be pointed out that the Western Asia Purchasing Director had not just advised caution, but basically stated this was a really bad idea and not throw money away. Smelling a "victory" over the Purchasing team and seeing an East victory over the West the said Sales Director then went through the process of ensuring a payment was made by internet to this company found on the internet. So the next day expecting to cement the victory at 1pm the Sales Director tried raising the supplier on the phone…... 1pm became 2pm, which became 3pm……. Surprisingly enough the phone calls were never answered, nor were the emails and funnily enough when they finally thought to try and stop the monies the account of the company had already closed, some $5,000 better off than they had been the day before. Unfortunately, or more realistically, this was an inevitable outcome. On a positive note the Sales Director didn't feel guilty about having just posted $5,000 to someone for nothing……it wasn't their money anyway......

– Hiring of personnel is time consuming, frustrating and in the majority of cases ends in failure – across all functions. A key requirement often for interview was candidates being able to speak English. On receipt of CVs in Chinese I requested an English version. These would arrive and interviews would be set up. At the time of the interview I would go the meeting room, only for the HR Manager to come in and tell me not to bother... as the candidate did not speak a word of English.

– Securing TS16949 is clearly significantly less challenging in China than the rest of the world.

Getting quality accreditation can be very simple, especially in comparison to Europe and North America. The auditors, who are from the same company used in the West, clearly had radically different standards to those auditors from the West. There is categorically no way the company would have got its TS re-certification if it had been audited by a western auditor. One of the pre-requisites for such accreditation is you have a documented system and traceability to show you are following the said system. The clue, in this case, is the fact you need to have a system......

– Implementation of any ERP system can NOT be done with inexperienced persons.

Having finally made the decision, a year too late, to implement the standard company ERP system, the integration team was made up of a mix of people with limited business and process knowledge, and a fair sprinkling of people who did not want the system to change, as they wouldn't be able continue with some of their extra-curricular activities. The ERP system should have been housed in the Wuxi facility with management and maintained from there, with just the capability to generate supplier schedules and enter receipts in Shanghai. Not only would it have protected the fundamental structure of the bills of materials, it would also have avoided an even bigger mess when eventually the Shanghai facility was closed and moved. It was yet another example of a correct idea not being thought through and the continued denial from parts of the business that could not comprehend the realities of life on the ground.

− If we cannot make it in house just ~~ask~~ tell a supplier, they have to do it.

Normally Make V Buy decisions were made to out-source based on a lack of timing on a programme. Invariably the decision to "buy" focused on the more complex parts in the product that needed the highest level of focus and attention and would be seen as "core competence". These were the exact parts and sub-assemblies which should be manufactured and controlled in house. Outsourcing them was, simply put, a way to relinquish responsibility, but it also turned out to be a key element in 'planning for failure', but that then became 'Someone' else's issue.

− Requests to support Europe, predominately on supplier issues affecting Europe, could not be handled effectively by the infrastructure in China.

The skill levels and resources were just not there. The spoken English of the team was weak, the technical skill set of the team was poor and was typical of the attitude towards purchasing per se.

There were generally three categories of purchasing people. The good ones tend to be older and have been in other functions like engineering and could actually add value, unfortunately they are very unlikely to speak English. Those that speak English tend to have no experience, and if you could find one with good English and capable would certainly be taking hongbao's.

– All business is done on trust and relationship (guan shi) rather than facts and documented agreements.

Trust is a very important part of business activity in China, however the Chinese seem to have a huge mistrust of other Chinese people in business. It's a huge oxymoron for sure, but written contracts seem to have little or no value. Do not expect that just because you have a confidentiality agreement in place with a company they will not be discussing your product with your competitor.

– If sleeping was an Olympic sport, the employees at the Shanghai facility would have had a facility full of Gold medallists.

As soon as there was a break, for example lunch, the employees would eat and then go and find some cardboard packaging to make an impromptu bed. At lunchtime in the offices the lights would be turned out and there would be a mass sleep in at the desks. Nothing happened during these breaks, literally nothing.

– Internal communication between the local management and employees 'necessitated' contacting a western manager first, rather than walk five paces and ask the person directly.

The communication process only seemed to happen when a western person was first communicated with. No matter what it related to, for example needing people for a meeting, the request first was made to the westerner. It was about appearing to be more important than going directly to approach the western head of a function first.

– Software licences in the Shanghai facility were 80% illegal copies, despite monies being sanctioned to buy legitimate copies.

Illegal software, corrupt and incompatible files were also very common. I am convinced Mr McAfee must have made his fortune off our western facilities receiving corrupt files from the Shanghai facility. At the same time many of the westerners had their machines hacked into and data stolen. If work needed to be carried out on your laptop it should never be let out of sight. Hanging around IT was worthwhile, even if you weren't an expert, as it was unlikely they would implant any software you could not recognise if you were present.

The average age of a PC in the facility was eight years old, giving people an extra excuse for not being able to supply information. For some reason PCs were not updated. It was never clear why this was, but when someone left the replacement employee would inherit a machine that was just not capable of performing the necessary tasks. Although employees used this as an excuse not to work, it wasn't their fault they had bad equipment. Virtually all PCs in the facility were ones that had been sent from overseas, where the policy was to replace a machine every three years. An interesting concept...."this equipment is not good enough for us….but it's good enough for China"!

− In excess of RMB 8,300,000 ($1,400,000) of annual business had been transferred from in-house or sister companies to snake suppliers during the period from 31 December 2007 to 30 September 2009.

− This on its own is not illegal. You could argue it as illogical, until documentation was uncovered that showed the product price increased by 30% from the previous level. In essence the snakes pocketed over $400,000 a year by changing to their family-owned supply base. Not a bad return if you can get it…..who said nepotism isn't good for you….!!!!

At the same time production equipment from the shop floor literally disappeared overnight. In one specific case I actually found the equipment installed at one of the snake-owned external companies. I was able to prove this as they had forgotten to remove the asset tags. The snakes then produced a fabricated letter stating they had been given permission to take the assets. No monetary value was made for the transfers and there were no documents internally agreeing to or allowing such a transfer. I am sure their lawyers printer could have been linked to that case as well……

− Implementation of a global eProcurement tool and process in 2008 would have removed the possibility of non-performing or incapable suppliers being selected for new projects. Ultimately it would have sped up the company's ability to get control of its suppliers and data.

Such a tool would have allowed the company very carefully to manage its supplier base and remove the potential and actual corruption that was taking place with the existing suppliers. For example, one of the plastic injection moulding companies used was run by the brother-in-law of the head snake. This company supplied in the region of 650 different references for the facility. The facility used to supply the resin to them free of charge – as the supplier stated they were not able to get the required grades of materials themselves….. The supplier then used the material for moulding the parts and shipping them back. I was intrigued why the supplier was always running short of resin. There were a number of logical reasons:

1) The bills of materials could have been wrong therefore we could have been consuming more material than technically we should have been
2) There could have been higher levels of scrap being generated than forecasted. This is very possible due to the poor manufacturing and build quality of the tools
3) The suppliers were delivering less material than advised on their shipping and receiving documents. This was less likely…but definitely not impossible

On investigation I found two very simple explanations. Firstly the supplier was using our free issued resin to produce parts for a competitor and secondly the supplier was using our free issued resin on our tools to supply parts to the said competitor….. The supplier, when I questioned them on this, openly admitted they were using our tools to produce the competitor's parts. It was not even a hidden process they were open and brazen about it.

– Business was stolen by snake companies.

A major local customer was very surprised one day when we visited them to discuss getting a particular piece of business. The supplier was very surprised to find out that we had originally been supplying them. The snake company had, for a number of years, been making sales to our customer with our product but had manipulated the invoice to say it came from them. How could you miss this from your own sales and reporting? Clearly there were still internal snakes operating and manipulating the books.

Another practice that happened until it was identified and a stop put to it was sales people charging the customer for 100 parts, when they asked for 80. The other 20 parts they made in essence were for free, these where then sold to the aftermarket for a huge mark up. On two counts this was totally illegal, however this did not seem to worry the sales people. So having put a written instruction out there for this to stop with immediate effect, it was picked up in an operations meeting six months later that the practice had continued. The Sales Manager was sacked, however I am very sure he was a very happy, and significantly richer, individual when he left the building.

– In sourcing any products that were being manufactured by snake companies took for ever to happen.

Stalling tactics were used in many different ways and techniques. There was a clear reason for this as obviously it would impact their free cash generation of $400,000 per annum. Getting to this process was also a little more than just challenging. The individuals who were benefiting from the free cash were very unhappy when someone came along and cut the power lead to the ATM. There were lots of physical threats made by employees and suppliers to a colleague and myself. The bullet hole in the office window showed that some of the local benefactors were really not happy at all. Fortunately they were about as capable with a gun as they were in making stuff.

– Quality of information communicated was extremely poor. It was time consuming actually to find out any 'issue' and even more time consuming to fix, due to other associated issues being identified during the investigation.

Dealing with issues in the facility was a little bit like peeling an onion. Peel the outer layer and then you exposed the next layer, and the next layer and the next layer etc. For example an issue relating to paying a supplier would take you back to the matching process, which would take you back to the receipt and the invoice submission, the raising of the purchase order and who actually then ordered the materials in question. At each stage a number of other issues would arise and after a while it was very difficult to remember what had actually started the original issue as it had created 50 smaller issues all needing to be fixed.

– The lease on the Shanghai facility was renegotiated after the acquisition process had been completed.

The owner of the facility was the head snake. The person who negotiated the new deal was a senior member of the old company management team who had been part of the sale programme. He was also very closely associated with the head snake. The new lease contract stated that if our company wanted to exit the building, it was terminated on a twelve month period basis. If the head snake wanted us out he had to provide a three month notice period. Speculation of how much the signature on that contract cost is still unclear, but for sure it would have been worth his while.

– The Asia Purchasing Director (son in law of the head snake) also turned out to be the landlord for the dormitories we rented for the workers.

It is fairly normal for companies to provide dormitories for its workers. 90% of the shop floor employees were migrant workers. They were housed very close to the facility, and it was only uncovered he was the landlord when he was sacked. These dormitories housed 700 people, so it was a real question to know where he found the money to buy buildings big enough to house 700 people... Amazing what a company salary of $4,500 per month could buy you.

The Asia Purchasing Director was pretty upset the day he was fired, mainly because we took his company laptop off him. He claimed the company laptop was a personal gift from his predecessor who had headed up the Asia Purchasing Team and was an American expatriate. After we had the contents of the laptop examined it was pretty clear why he was upset. It provided some very interesting insight into his financial matters, along with confidential information the western management team had been working on in relation to the changes being planned to recover the situation. This information had only been shared by that group of people.....or so we thought. There was a person working in one of our French facilities closely associated with the ex-Asia Purchasing Director who had got sight, from the French VP of Purchasing. The French VP of Purchasing refused to believe the facts of what was being reported from China and circulated the confidential information...

– Knee jerk reactions were commonplace and purely based around customer demands, which in themselves were knee jerk reactions.

One evening we received a complaint from a customer who said a welded rod assembly was failing under a torque test. This seemed very strange. However, rather than making an investigation and doing a root cause analysis, the Plant Manager, who was local Chinese, decided to summon the supplier to tell him how bad he was and ordered him overnight to change the raw material to a harder one. The next morning the supplier started shipping production with a harder material. There was no documentation to support this change, and he did not think it important enough to tell engineering, purchasing or the western President. A day later the same issue came up. All the stocks at the customer had been collected, so the General Manager decided to go for an even harder material. The process was repeated. The customer gladly charged us all the costs associated with shipping the goods, rework costs etc. On the third day we found out about it and sat in a meeting in stunned silence at his actions. He was actually pleased with what he had done to support the customer. Having suggested to him to re-insert his brain from his arse, we asked the customer if they had changed anything in their process. The answer came back, "Yes, we have removed the fixture holding the rod in place whilst doing the torque test…" I still do not know how, but the General Manager was not fired. Nor was he fired for changing a patented product he ran out of that could only be sourced from a company in North America. Rather than telling me, he decided to switch to a local manufacturer, and for a whole month product was being shipped and sold in Europe that had never been tested or validated internally, let alone gone to a customer. I actually only found out because the correct supplier rang me to ask what had happened to his orders!

− Capital equipment obsolescence and subsequent sale has been poorly managed. Moulding machines, ultrasonic welders and presses were sitting in an obsolete area whilst new equipment was been purchased.

There was literally a graveyard of capital equipment sitting in an off-site warehouse. It took me a whole week to hand truck this equipment from the third floor warehouse and get it loaded onto trucks to be sold for scrap. Where it came from and why it was there, no one knew….. I still have not managed to meet this 'no one'. They certainly have a lot to answer for.

− European support to train personnel was ineffective and simply ignored, due mainly to poor communication and no follow up.

People sent over to support the transition process were rarely there out of choice. They wanted to get in and out as soon as possible. Whilst they knew what needed to be done, it was very clear they were not going to support the changes by dedicating time to being there and additionally the locals did not particularly want to learn. The maximum a westerner was likely to spend helping out was three months. Three months was a real cut off point mainly because up to that point a person from continental Europe would get a daily overseas supplementary monetary rate. The support we had always came from the countries that were paying $120 per day to cover meals and general inconvenience. So after twelve weeks and being $11,000 tax free better off, the caring, sharing resource would head back home claiming the hardships of living and working there had drained them physically and emotionally…!!!

– Data provided for month-end reports of quality measures completely hid the reality.

Supplier Part Per Million (PPM – a measure if the number of defective parts supplied) of 250 were complete fabrications. Supplier PPM's of 250 with 900 open supplier claims were an oxymoron. A Best in Class company will strive to deliver to zero PPM, however this is a virtual impossibility to achieve on the complex systems most automotive suppliers manufacture. Certainly in comparable businesses in the West supplier PPM's would normally be in the region of 300 to 500. To achieve this level of performance it would be impossible to have 900 open supplier issues. Each open issue is, or should be, controlled by an 8D.

Note of explanation - Eight Disciplines Problem Solving (8D) is a method used to approach and to resolve problems. Its purpose is to identify, correct and eliminate recurring problems, and it is useful in product and process improvement. It establishes a permanent corrective action based on statistical analysis of the problem and focuses on the origin of the problem by determining its root causes. Although it originally comprised eight stages, or 'disciplines', it was later augmented by an initial planning stage. The disciplines are:

D0: **Plan**: Plan for solving the problem and determine the prerequisites.

D1: **Use a Team**: Establish a team of people with product/process knowledge.

D2: Define and describe the Problem: Specify the problem by identifying in quantifiable terms the who, what, where, when, why, how, and how many (5W2H) for the problem.

D3: Develop Interim Containment Plan; Implement and verify Interim Actions: Define and implement containment actions to isolate the problem from any customer.

D4: Determine, Identify, and Verify Root Causes and Escape Points: Identify all applicable causes that could explain why the problem has occurred. Also identify why the problem has not been noticed at the time it occurred. All causes shall be verified or proved, not determined by fuzzy brainstorming.

D5: Choose and Verify Permanent Corrections (PCs) for Problem/Non Conformity: Through pre-production programs quantitatively confirm that the selected correction will resolve the problem for the customer. (Verify the correction will actually solve the problem)

D6: Implement and Validate Corrective Actions: Define and Implement the best corrective actions.

D7: Take Preventive Measures: Modify the management systems, operation systems, practices, and procedures to prevent recurrence of this and all similar problems.

D8: Congratulate Your Team: Recognize the collective efforts of the team. The team needs to be formally thanked by the organization.

8D has become a standard in the auto, assembly and other industries that require a thorough structured problem solving process using a team approach

This again goes back to the lack of ability to trace information. Any manual system is going to be at risk of error as people are only 80% efficient. Add into that there was no desire by locals to make this work. It was a case of putting some numbers on a piece of paper that no westerner would be able to confirm or deny. The irony is that the data provided by these people was so wildly incompatible they caught themselves out!

Purchasing

– Tooling ownership and traceability was non-existent.

Customers had paid for the majority of tooling, if not all, but the suppliers were never paid! Where did the money go? Where was the traceability?

There are many reasons to be careful when buying tooling in China. Can the quality be good? Absolutely, however, you need to be totally on top of the tool maker and fundamentally, explicitly clear and understood what the total specification is. Never allow for any assumptions otherwise you will end up with a split line right across an aesthetic face. Small note on the word 'assume'. There is a very good meaning... 'it makes an ASS of U and ME.' And in China it really will make an ass out of you, a very expensive one.

The real issue with tooling in China, specifically when you are paying a supplier for tooling that is going to produce and supply production parts to you, is the tooling generally looks very competitive against many other countries. There is a real allure of price, but not what is behind it. Generally what you are paying for with your tooling cost is a tool to manufacture a year's worth of product. Included in your part price is also an amortisation cost – which they use to cover the cost of producing a second tool in year two and a third in year three etc.

If you are buying tooling to use in house the challenges are no less severe. Raising a purchase order and then waiting for the supplier to meet the timeline is planning for disappointment. Not only will you be disappointed in the timing, you will, unless you are omnipresent, be disappointed in the quality. A major programme was launched with tooling for eventual supply to a USA OEM. The tooling arrived, was inspected, and then promptly sent to a local tool maker to try and turn it to a set of tooling that could be used to meet the requirements. Twelve months later the tooling was spending more time in repair shops than it was in the presses. When they were in the presses it resulted in 24/7 working and significant scrap levels. The moral of this tale is consider total acquisition cost and not get dazzled by the initial "price".

However back to the supplier tooling used by themselves..... Additionally suppliers kind of forget to advise you they have started production with a new tool. Many a quality engineer in Europe or the Americas sits there checking parts not able to understand why all of a sudden the part dimensions have changed... not that they were correct before... Then the engineer finds the tell-tale sign of true Chinese incompetence. Instead of hiding their unauthorised practice they forget, on the new tool, to mark up the cavities, which had been a clear stipulation on the first set and were clearly visible on all parts. Once the cat is out of the bag they will come up with all the excuses on the planet why it is the same tool, until they finally admit it's a second tool and the first one had worn out!

Having set the scene the specific challenge faced at the Shanghai facility was that the moulding company, owned by a relative of the head snake, held in excess of 600 different tools of ours. When the joint venture ended, the fact I had sacked a close relative, and half the snakes that had left our company were working there, created some challenges. We had documented evidence the Shanghai facility had sold the tools at the start of the programme, some three years previously, to a sister facility in France. All the records from the facility were missing and there was no proof that the supplier had been paid for the tools. After doing a major internal financial forensic analysis it was possible to prove that a sum of monies amounting to the value of the tools had in fact been paid to the supplier. There could be no other logical explanation, but still not proof. The supplier continued to state they had never been paid for the tools. Then came a lucky break. Hidden in the head snake's 'private office' I found a treasure trove of 'lost' files. Amongst this were a number of records relating to some of the tooling the supplier claimed had never been paid for. The supplier continued to protest their innocence advising they had never been paid for them. Due to running them around in circles I had been able to get a statement and clearly documented quotations that on other tooling they supplied us they amortised into the piece part price an element of the tooling. Still they would not back down. Twelve months later we reached an agreement where we were able to get our asset tags put onto the tools and at last could prove ownership. The final cost of that agreement:

1) Payment of the tooling up front
2) Four years of tooling amortisation and
3) A haggled ownership transfer cost fee.

The total value of the agreement was in the region of $3,000,000 and in essence the company had paid for the initial tooling cost three times over....... On the positive side, there were at least four sets of all tools!

− The number of suppliers tooling had been laid down with was unknown.

A specific programme was decided, after we took full

ownership, to be transferred to Europe. During the process of building up the plan and organising the tooling for transfer to Europe, a number of situations arose where it came to light that two or more suppliers had laid down tooling for the same part number without any tooling commitment. On top of this deliveries had been received from all these sub suppliers at some time, and it was simply impossible to trace who had supplied what. So back we went to the PPAP's…..errr OK….. Let's move on…….

- Knowing your suppliers.

The Purchasing Manager of the Shanghai facility, who had been with the company for seven years, had never visited a single supplier. Nor for that matter had any other member of the purchasing department. It's also questionable if any supplier quality personnel had visited any supplier.

Some of the local purchasing team were too intimidated to go to the snake companies and were clearly warned off going there. On a number of occasions the ASQ personnel refused to visit suppliers. After the third occasion they were released, fortunately by this time a new Asia Purchasing Director had joined, who was a western expatriate. He recruited a new Team of Buyers and ASQ from outside of Shanghai and the results were interesting putting it mildly. Even the new personnel were shocked with what they uncovered…..

As a note on this, I knew this new Purchasing Director very well and, for three months prior to him arriving I had called him regularly to tell him what was going on. Calls would last an hour or more pretty much most days. He listened and listened. After three months living in Shanghai, he turned around to me one evening and said, "I listened to everything you told me on those calls, but I just didn't believe you. It could not be possible... I really should have believed you."

– All supplier sourcing and nomination was made by the head snake's son-in-law.

Due to the hierarchical structure in China, and the complete power the head snake had over the business, no one would dare question a decision. Additionally, for the shop floor employees it's a very long way back home, literally. With no money and basically nowhere to live, going against the head snake's will would not have been a thought that entered their heads lightly. The migrant workers would basically go back home once a year or maybe once every two years at the time of the Chinese New Year. Beyond that they were in essence slaves of the head snake.

– China sourcing for sister facilities overseas

The company had a number of years before, set up an Asian sourcing office in Shanghai which in essence was there to look after the overseas sourcing of products. The head of that department was a westerner who was known as 'having retired on active service'. His approach was to delegate the day-to-day running to his second in command, who was the same son-in-law of the head snake who went on to become the next Asia Purchasing Director. His second in command was manipulated into this position by the Fixer. What a perfect solution for Mr Retired On Active Service. He could go and play as much golf as he wanted, not having to worry about life as his second in command was supported by the Fixer and the head boss of the Division in the West....... He definitely fell into the first category of People referred to earlier – "Some will allow things to happen that shouldn't". He and I spoke on a number of occasions and he was aware things were not right, but accepted the situation and kept his head down. Considering where the bulk of the manufacturing and other activities were out of the three Shanghai facilities the company had, he strategically had placed his office nowhere near the action

In essence all European supplier sourcing and selection from China was done by the head snake's son-in-law. Additionally to lining the pockets of his father-in-law's companies – and for sure his own, something had to be paying for those flats he was renting out – he also was able to gather huge amounts of confidential business information which was passed onto our competitors. Could we prove it? Well actually yes, as when we confiscated his laptop it contained all the information that would constitute proof – at least to a court in the West.

– Purchase order traceability was non-existent.

There was no accountability and everything was signed off by a high profile snake. There was not just corruption going on the simple fact was that the local process for ordering goods and services was a verbal one. The paper was only there as it was occasionally necessary for the company to allow some auditor in to take a look at the 'official' set of books. Any system can be corrupted, however, to allow such a manual processes is creating a significantly higher risk that could otherwise have been avoided. Putting this into perspective and into the context of corruption as a whole, corruption does not have to be for massive sums of monies. Consider this, an invoice is received for 10 different parts numbers and there is a difference on it from the prices on the purchase order. The total order value should be $25,000 and it comes in at $25,125.75. With the manual processes in place and the physical number of invoices being sent in, the Finance Department would submit this variance to be paid. The payment would be made and a logistics supervisor would have just made an additional week's wages. Well the order was verbal, so were the original prices really correct, and it was only $125.75???.........

Another example of this, with slightly more significant sums involved. Invoices were paid by matching an invoice against an advice note and occasionally a purchase order. The practice sounds good, but the person who did the matching was the material controller, the same one that was ordering steel and signing for two tonnes, when in fact only one was actually shipped. The one that walked out of the company – OK, was actually fired for pulling a knife on our finance Director in the office – left $100,000 better off after just six months at the company, on a salary of $600 per month. When the western Asia Purchasing Director arrived they made him an authority to release funds to pay the suppliers. He had to go physically into the company bank account and transfer monies. So someone from finance would come to him and tell him he needed urgently to process invoices and release the monies so suppliers could be paid. The first time this happened he obliged. Next week exactly the same thing occurred. At the last minute the finance person came along again. This time he questioned why. Realising that he was not going to release funds without an answer she left with the unpaid invoices. Next week the same again, with the same result. The suppliers, theoretically, by now should have been screaming, but someone else had managed to get a key to enter the bank account. Every time a request came to him he questioned the invoices, the values and so on. After six

months they took the key from him, saying he was being too difficult! Even the company CFO contacted him to ask him why he was not releasing payments……
Refer back to corporate seagulls…..

– Supplier quotations (QAFs) either did not exist (majority of cases) or were irrelevant.

The majority of pricing information was a single sheet of paper from the supplier that basically called up a part number, if there was one, or just a description with a price. There was no traceability back to a drawing or specification or revision level. There would be no form of price breakdown and categorically it would not reference any terms and conditions of purchase. A simple question here would be how could you actually reject anything to a supplier when there was no correlation from what you think you asked for to what the suppliers actually sent in? Somehow we managed it…..refer back to the 900 open issues that mysteriously disappeared…..

– Supplier PPAPs were not prepared or followed correctly, resulting in significant production related issues.

The Supplier Quality (SQ) function was 'poor' and incompetent. The concept of suppliers completing paperwork correctly was clearly a concept suppliers found very strange and generally was accepted by the SQ function. The correct completion and submission of DFMEA, PFEMA etc was a concept too far.

DFEMA - **Design Failure Mode and Effects Analysis** is the application of the Failure Mode and Effects Analysis method specifically to product design. It is a paper-and-pencil analysis method used in engineering to document and explore ways that a product design might fail in real-world use. A DFMEA documents the key functions of a design, the primary potential failure modes relative to each function and the potential causes of each failure mode. The DFMEA method allows the design team to document what they know and suspect about a product's failure modes prior to completing the design, and then use this information to design out or mitigate the causes of failure.

A PFMEA is similar to the above but used for the manufacturing Process of the product. It involves reviewing as many components, assemblies, and subsystems as possible to identify failure modes, and their causes and effects. For each component, the failure modes and their resulting effects on the rest of the system are recorded in a specific PFMEA worksheet. There are numerous variations of such worksheets.

Generally the latest technology of 'copy and paste' was employed. It was very common to see PPAP submissions from suppliers with the same information repeated on every part, and in a number of cases they did not even change the part number, so PPAP were submitted against the wrong part number!

– Supplier PPAP management was a joke, with products being signed off having significant numbers of non-conforming measurements.

Internal verification was basically non-existent. The fact we had received a PPAP at all meant it was another piece of paper to be filed as it was another tick in the box. Parts were assembled, with challenges, as invariably they were not to print and it only became an issue when the customer could not physically use the parts we shipped them. Prior to the termination of the joint venture this was not really an issue. The customer ASQ was given the right amount of hongbao and the issue went away. Overnight from the closure of the joint venture the quality performance from the facility went from zero PPM to thousands of PPM, as we stopped paying the hongbao's.

− Where PPAPs were signed off with deviations, drawings released for production were not modified.

With the snake moulding company there were at any point in time 300 engineering change requests (ECR) open. In essence the parts being shipped by the supplier could never be in line with the prints we were 'technically' inspecting to.

− Tooling asset registers were non-existent.

One business fundamental is being able to identify where your assets are at any given point in time. This is pretty simple when it comes to a factory, they simply don't move around (well that's not completely true − we did have one factory where the joint-venture partner in Shenzhen actually moved the factory without telling anyone. We had people going to visit the factory only to find it wasn't there).

Tooling however is very easily transferred, and it is vital that you have a strong control over where it is at all times. Normally that tooling is paid for ultimately by your customer and in essence they could pull that tooling from you at any time. Usually they don't, but technically they could. Either way it's a pretty important thing to have, as to supply your customer you need to know where your tools are etc. Walking into the Shanghai facility there were zero traceability of where our tool were. It was literally a case of asking suppliers to own up and then getting the tools asset tagged. Clearly the ones who saw dollar signs in front of their eyes were adamant that they had never been paid for the tooling, however in the vast majority of case it was possible to prove we had so seeing their quick gain disappear, they played ball. Just one recommendation when you do lay down tooling. Don't just get an asset tag on it, but make sure you photograph the tooling in the open condition and also get the supplier to sign a tool loan contract. Make sure you can really show it's the tooling you brought and signed off.

– At no point during the ordering process of direct materials was there a link with an issue level on a print. Technically the Shanghai facility could not accept or reject anything.

This is a really common process you will find in most local Chinese companies. At one point we actually had four different release levels of the same print in four locations simultaneously. The supplier had a version that was newer than our own engineering department had. The purchasing group had another issue level, as did the quality department, which was continuously rejecting the parts…..

– Tooling development was non-existent.

This was seen as the 'supplier's responsibility'. Design and manufacturing feasibility reviews were replaced by continuous trimming of tools, after manufacture, due to a lack of knowledge and experience internally. By the time a tool was in production it looked like a 'frankentool'. It would generally have more weld in it than original metal, and resultantly it was pure luck if parts could be produced even close to what was needed.

– Supplier changes were made without Customer knowledge or agreement. Applicable to both internal and external Customers.

It was technically and physically impossible to know what level of product was being shipped to a customer. Changes could happen on the shop floor at the time of assembly due to the erratic capability of the supplied child parts. I mentioned before about the changes the General Manager made on two key products without communication. There was a real belief that anything the customer said must be true. The concept of reviewing an issue to understand the root cause was never considered, it was only 'we have to keep the customer happy no matter what'. This naïve mentality cost the company thousands if not millions of dollars over the years.

– The purchasing department wanted to go on strike over pay and overtime.

Straight after the closure of the joint venture it's safe to say there was a dirty tricks campaign waged by the head snake. His goal was simply to bring the business to its knees so he could pick up all the work and take it to his new willing victim partner in Chongqing. On a number of occasions I crossed mass picket lines and we ended up allocating one of our offices to the local police precincts as they spent more time in our factory that on the streets. One day the complete purchasing team walked into the office demanding a mass pay rise and better overtime conditions. The statement from the western Asia Purchasing Director was great. "Please shut the door on your way out and when you leave the factory grounds shut the gate behind you." Unfortunately they all went back to work.

As a point of note here China is recognised for its employees working excessive overtime. There is a reason for this as the vast majority of Chinese make double their salaries by working overtime. One of my responsibilities was running the logistics function and every month I received the overtime hours worked report for approval. Workers would average between 80 and 100 hours per month. Believe it or not there is actually a law in China – as in the vast majority of countries – relating to the maximum amount of overtime that can be worked in a month. In China the legal maximum is 35 hours per month. This is not a company rule it is the law. The reality like many things in life over there, it depends on who you are whether you follow the rules or not.

– Suppliers often refused to talk to me as I wasn't their usual point of contact.

Don't be surprised at this. Suppliers normally have only one or two customers, and whoever has introduced them becomes the only contact they're prepared to work with. Whilst title in China is hugely important, it does not interfere with the relationship of the people who started that specific business activity. I think it's easy to understand why.

– Nine hundred open supplier claims zero in three week!

How exactly did this happen? We clearly had an issue, and it was with the supplier base. Well yes and no….OK should add maybe…. Parts would be supplied that were fundamentally the wrong dimension, and drawings needed updating. A list as long as this would normally take 18 months to two years to clear, if you were lucky. It was done in three weeks......err I don't think so..... Just another example of the continual and blatant lying along with the non-adherence to systems and processes.

– The introduction of a new ordering / invoice system, with supplier meetings in January, was implemented at the snake moulding supplier... in the October.

There was huge internal resistance and additionally poor supplier feedback. There was no form of forecasting or scheduling being used in the company. The basis of ordering was literally the material controller ringing the supplier and advising how many parts were ready or could be ready by such and such a time. Tool changes as a result happened on a continuous basis and we ended up totally hand-to-mouth with supply of parts. When twelve month rolling schedules were provided there was a reluctance to implement internally and at the suppliers and the idea of a Kanban supply (a pull system of inventory management) was doomed to failure for many reasons, one being the re-usable packaging required rapidly went missing... Why would there be such reluctance to implement? Simply due to the snake influences internally and with the key suppliers in question. Their goal of de-stabilisation could work mainly due to the number of issues that were being created and initially the reluctance to accept this could or would happen. Our colleagues in the West were continuing to look at business dealings in exactly the same way it would be done in their part of the world

– Recognition of name change in supplier tooling was

slow and outside the contracted window.

With a company name change, many alterations had to happen from the signage outside and on the buildings to the tooling name embossed on the child parts. In the due diligence process there was a clearly defined grace time to get this completed, six months. In reality it took closer to three years to get all tools changed, and no matter what pressure was brought the process just stagnated. Our previous owner technically could have sued us after the grace period and up until the changes were implemented. It's highly likely they would have done if they were more smart in this situation, specifically as we were notifying them of our intention to sue due to the issues that had manifested themselves after the takeover.

– Suppliers contacted and chased the Shanghai facility to pay for tooling manufactured prior to the sale of company during the time it was a joint venture.

As part of the due diligence work information like this should have been disclosed prior to the sale. Additionally outstanding balances should have been taken into consideration in the sale price. If however you accidentally....or was that deliberately???....choose not to disclose information then you leave yourself open to be sued

Normally you would associate this process with maybe some phone calls, letters and then ultimately receiving a summons from a lawyer via a court. This isn't the normal process in China. Instead, someone turns up and demands money from the westerners. When you say 'mayo' (no), they go away and the next day a few more of them turn up demanding the monies. You say no again. The next day they come along with the 'heavies' and start threatening. So you say no again and they wait for you outside the factory gates… with the 'heavies'. Fortunately both the western Asia Purchasing Director and I were not small people and their heavies, whilst I am sure were capable, did not really fancy getting into a fist fight with two westerners. The verbal and physical threats went on for a period of three to four months. During that time the company hired the services of a professional overseas security company to keep an eye on us and help us with the investigations into the extremely poor business practices and in reality the corruption. It was comforting to know there were people you could call on.

–   Whilst 70% of the Shanghai facility spend was with known snake companies, *all* suppliers there had been set up by the snakes, therefore potentially 100% were snake suppliers.

The relevance here is that when faced with blatant corrupt practices you look for alternatives. The other, let's say, "quiet suppliers" are generally the ones you would go to. Unfortunately they could also be there to be seen as playing the 'good cop' and ultimately you end up transferring business from a corrupt known company to one where the snakes are still getting their income and you unwittingly have recommended them to the rest of the organisation.

On this subject it is an important sub note in relation to China per say. When you arrive in the country, generally as a westerner you cannot speak the language, nor read the signs. On the roads there are many western spelt road names, however this will not really help you get from A to B. Getting back to the language, however, you are immediately faced with a challenge, one that's resolved by the first person you meet who speaks English. The vast majority of people arriving for the first time will make the same mistake, and it can be very costly. Consciously or sub-consciously you will trust that person. The fact they can help you is a significant relief and you immediately go off your guard. Not only are you vulnerable, you tend to be gullible. Why? Simply put you have not had the opportunity to readjust your values to where you are. Be careful about falling into this trap and from day one make sure you use the triangulation question process – asking three questions, saying the same thing three different ways, and see if you get the same answer.

– Suppliers were changed after start of production (SOP), without customer validation and approval. This could be widely seen across a range of programmes.

It all relates back to the lack of disciple and following procedures. It plays right into my earlier point about this being the nation that patented the phrase 'short cut'.

Logistics

– Freight controls were none existent.

19 different freight providers were being used each month and all freight costs were being picked up by the Shanghai facility. On investigation we found out that a number of these companies we were working with were simply fake ones who had been introduced as 'brokers', when in reality some were actually employees who had been able to present themselves to actual freight providers as our logistics broker. In simple terms they were creating an invoice with a 10% to 30% mark-up of the actual freight pricing and then signing the invoices for payment – which would invariably be paid as a small appreciation gesture would be handed over on a monthly basis. Again this was just clear deception, and in reality if there had not been so much greed involved, would probably not have been raised to the radar level it was.

– The Shanghai facility was a $45 million business with no ERP system, no inventory management and no effective quality control system.

The personnel did not want to implement any system – was this job preservation? I use the term job preservation very loosely. It was more they did not want the free cash line to end. It was to all intents and purposes like going to an ATM and not putting in a card or a code and getting money. With an effective ERP system in place it would have been significantly more difficult for this practice to take place.

– The definition of 'consignment stock' in Shanghai

was to get the supplier to deliver a quantity of goods and then notify them some time later what they could invoice.

The notification was controlled directly by the logistics department and was fully open to bribery. There was no secure controlled area for this 'consignment stock' and no traceability of what had been delivered and when. Two years after the company exited the joint venture and was sold they were still receiving demands relating to 'consignment stock' materials, where suppliers had never been allowed to invoice for goods supplied. The majority of the suppliers who contacted us had been put up to it by the head snake, again as part of his de-stabilisation process.

– Bills of materials were stored in two locations – the local Chinese ERP system and an Access database. Both were incorrect.

The Access database had in a number of cases been deliberately tampered with to ensure the facility ran out of materials, yet another example of the de-stabilising tactics from the head snake. Ultimately we had to get bill of material specialists from Europe to spend months in China to completely re-create all the bills of materials by taking existing products and stripping them down, once we had been able to confirm the part was actually complete.

– Logistics Managers recruitment

We hired two new Logistics Managers in one year. Both lasted fewer than 24 hours. Dead rats left in employee's drawers and threats to other members of the logistics staff did not help matters. Clearly the goal was to bring local external resources into the company to get the company back on track. We had to get rid of the remaining snakes and move forwards, however it was safe to say we all underestimated the powerful, persuasive and in many cases nasty ways people were intimidated. It was realistically only possible for us to protect the employees whilst they were on the site, intimidation doesn't just end at the factory walls. One young engineer ended up spending some time in hospital due to the fact he was seen as trying to help us get the business back on track.

– Logistics staff destabilisation

Some logistics people in the third floor off-site warehouse deliberately challenged the business with lack of kitting of parts. Due to business growth the original factory floor was not big enough to house the 'consignment stocks' from the suppliers. So within 500 metres of the factory an off-site warehouse had been established on the third floor of another company. The warehouse was serviced by two lifts that I'm sure were from the time before lifts had been invented. The warehouse itself was a dirty and dark building. Like pretty much all buildings in Shanghai it was less than ten years old. Any building past that age is generally considered as prime for either falling down or being pulled down. Building maintenance has yet to be invented in China.

A side note story here to put this into context. When I moved to Shanghai I was provided with an apartment in an area where a lot of ex-patriots lived. The apartment block, at that time was roughly 9 years old. On the surface the apartment was absolutely fine. Things generally worked and despite some challenges with falling through a floor in the underground garage into the sewer….everything seemed OK! Having been there for a couple of months I noticed a growing rancid smell coming from the kitchen area. I checked all the usual suspects – cupboards, fridge, cooker etc, very few of these areas were in use by me….especially not the cooker! The apartment was a serviced one so twice per week "someone" would clean it. Still the smell was getting stronger and stronger. I contacted the concierge and expressed my concerns. A maintenance person came and went….no resolution. So again I raised my concern and on a particular Saturday morning I was invaded by 8 maintenance and supervisors etc from the complex. At last they all agreed they could recognise the smell and it was by now hideous. So a maintenance guy sticks his head into a service vent in the roof and almost passes out. The culprit turned out to be the toilet waste pipe from the apartment above had been blocked and then cracked open and was spilling raw sewage directly into the gap between the floor of the above apartment and the roof of mine. The story has a happy ending, for me at least, as I very shortly moved out of the complex to an apartment that was only five years old….so hopefully still had had four years of life left in it before the smells returned……

So back to the third floor warehouse. There was no way to get fork lift trucks to this warehouse, so all materials were literally handballed on manual pallet trucks via the lifts. We even employed two people to man the lifts. Their 12 hour-a-day job was to push the button up and down. To give you a flavour of this warehouse it reminded me of the final scene from the film *Raiders of the Lost Ark*, where the Ark disappears into that huge warehouse and becomes lost. Well we had our own version. The area was 5,000 square metres and there was barely room to get hand trucks down isles. I personally removed over 100 tonnes of obsolete material from that warehouse using just a pump truck in a two day period. This may not sound impressive, but try doing it in 40 degree celsius temperatures and going up and down in the world's slowest lift. I certainly didn't need to go to the gym afterwards. Having removed the 100 tonnes of obsolete material you quite literally could not see what had changed. That obsolete material, out of interest, equated to over $500,000 that had to be written off. This should have been done prior to the sale of the company by the previous owners.

A final note on warehouses and use of, before getting real control over the warehousing the company had six separate external storage facilities with 'stuff' in them. I am really not sure what else you could call it. One of the external warehouses was full of PVC leather – something I recommended we sell to the local tailors, at least they might be able to make some jackets.....albeit the colours and styles would probably not be suitable to most people's tastes!

– Inventory management

Inventory from the snake companies was 'pushed' into the facility as opposed to being 'pulled' in from the others. Their ability to generate cash and profit was astounding and just the scale of it was difficult to deal with. The chaotic approach to warehousing of goods had literally got out of control. Just trying to identify where all of a particular part number was located could literally take days. In the meantime more inventory was received as 'no one' knew if we had any or not... Much consideration was given as to how to get control of the materials, including a simple two bin approach – example you have two bins on a shelf, when the first is empty, as you are using the contents from the second one, the first one is replaced. Simple but effective. But for a long time the efforts were frustrated by snakes that remained.

– Customer forecasts were never translated into supplier forecasts.

Changes in customer forecasts could take weeks to be implemented into the production plans – and therefore the supplier calls off. This was due to the manual tools and the fact the planning being controlled by individuals and not EDI systems.

Slow-moving and obsolete inventory was identified solely by the logistics department based on their experience. There was no interaction with any other parts of the business and it was by no mean complete, far from it. There were many examples of materials that were obsoleted and scrapped off being later mysteriously required for some product that had been "forgotten" about. I had "forgotten" that "forgotten" was another of the most popular surnames...... This was also relevant for capital equipment. The 'stuff' they didn't want was sent to the warehouse graveyard so they could have some new 'stuff'. Could the existing equipment have done the job? Absolutely!

Any business needs a strong base which is made up with controlled systems, people with good experience and knowledge of the products, customers and the ism's of how everything hangs together. To run a business without all of these different elements is planning for failure. There are reasons you have systems, procedures and tools, humans by their pure nature are only 80% effective, and that's when they are working with, not against, you.

Projects, Engineering and Design

– Programme launches and launch teams were poor and unmanaged.

The reality faced with was the only way a programme could be launched was if the westerners drove the programme. There were weekly programme management meetings. Like the other meetings I referred to earlier, the Programme Managers would turn up with their note books and pens, totally unprepared and not being able to answer any of the questions from the week before. It was a living version of *Groundhog Day*. Unfortunately for us Bill Murray was paid significantly more money for his version and it probably only took him three months of his life to complete.

– Programme Managers had a "world class" inability to be able to communicate

One more general comment here on communication, for the wider audience, if you work for a 'global' company. By that I mean a company that physically manufactures and operates on multiple continents, not just selling "stuff" in different parts of the world. Why does everyone think all timing is based on Eastern Standard Time? In the past 26 years I have yet to work for a company that actually consciously thinks about this or does anything about it, so let me explain what I mean. There are very few employees with company cell phones in China. Every employee has their own cell phone, if not more than one – very much like the rest of the global business world these days.

Some useless facts for you....Panama has the

highest number of cell phones per person in the world. On average every person in the country has just over two cell phones each (202% ownership). At the other end of the scale comes North Korea with a cell phone ownership of only 8.3% of the population. China has the most cell phones in the world at over 1.2 billion.....but only 89% of the population theoretically own them!!! Based on where they sit in the percentage stakes today I guess Apple, Nokia, Samsung and the others will be pretty much camped out in China for the foreseeable future. What's that saying from Orange the former UK owned service provider ..... "The futures bright.....the futures Orange". I guess someone might be changing the colour!

So back to Chinese business cell phones. Rather than give employees cell phones, companies give the employees an allocation of $15 to $20 per month so they will use their phones for company business. This sounds like a good idea, as there's no expense for the company buying and maintaining phones etc. The only minor flaws are that telephone calls outside of China cost an awful lot of money – unless you use the re-routing number (point of note to anyone not knowing: dial 12593 in front of your number - ie to dial Germany it would be 12593 0049 and then the rest of the number. It works and your costs reduce by significant amounts. The downside is that at certain times of the day you can't connect due to over use). The second flaw, linked to the first, and also significantly linked to this concept that time starts in EST, is that invariably conference calls with the rest of the world are done when North America wakes up, which believe it or not is night time in China. Just to clarify there is a 12 or 13 hour time difference depending on what time of the year to EST. To make this real simple if you schedule a call at 09:00 EST it's either 21:00 or 22:00 in China.

Now let me ask the question how many westerners are regularly prepared to attend a conference call at 21:00 or 22:00 at night? I'll give you the answer you already know… very few. Why? Well, "It's interfering with my personal time and the company has enough of me already…" etc. So rather than you being put out you would prefer to put someone else out, who isn't going to dial in anyway…… The fact the company gives the Chinese employees an allocation for phone calls is something that goes straight into their income and will never materialise into late night conference calls.

Another reality check: invariably the person organising the call won't consider the USA toll free number isn't applicable to anyone dialling in from outside the USA. The international number is just that. I was talking to one of our human resources directors a few years back. She used to occasionally dial into such meetings from her cell phone. Just to be on the call for one hour cost in excess of one hundred dollars.

So back to our local Chinese friends and their $20.00 per month allocation. Err the maths still doesn't add up and never will. If you want to get a Chinese person on a conference call you will either be running the call at 04:00 or 21:00 EST. The only way they will dial in is from a company land line……or alternatively you stand a better chance if you provided some company cell phones. Either way the other message here is that there is predominately a blatant disregard of other people and where they are located. It seems to be always about "self" and normally what is convenient for Corporate World. Written another way…..lack of cultural awareness.

– Design for manufacturing and process feasibility was non-existent. Skill levels were too low.

Generally when designing a product it's helpful to consider the question, "Can we make it?" It would be even better to consider, "Can we make it consistently and commercially viable?" Unfortunately neither of these concepts were thought through. Much of the process was based on how a product was built in the prototype shop. As for the design, it's always dangerous to ask an engineer to design something, as they are very keen to re-design something that is a proven product. The wheel is round for a purpose, so don't try and change it because you know how to use a CAD machine. In fact the CAD engineers might as well have been housed on Mars, as I don't think one of them knew where the shop floor was, or in fact why it was there.

– Project management was non-existent and the Project Management Manager was a compulsive liar.

There were people in the company with this title, however it was clear they had no concept of what the job actually entailed, and clearly had no competence to do the role. I am frequently heard to use the phrase, "If you have a headache do you call a plumber?" There are so many occasions where this is applicable – a more recent example I can give you is an EVP of the sales department deciding he was going to create a global purchasing structure. Would you allow your local doctor to perform open heart surgery? They are a medical practitioner, isn't that good enough…..? Why is it that so many organisations go for someone with no experience in a field, provide no training and then wonder why it does not deliver the expected outcome? This links directly back to the project managers in the Shanghai facility.

As for the Manager of the area, the vote was out

from day one if he was a snake, or just a compulsive liar. In the end the vote went to compulsive liar. He repeatedly went to customers and told them exactly what they wanted to hear, even though what he said could not have been further from the truth. As bad as it is to tell any Customer this the absolute worst is to try this approach with Japanese customers. For anyone not having dealt with the Japanese in business – specifically the car makers – they are truly proceduralised and very, very detailed. When they come to visit it's never for a day, a week maybe, but never anything shorter. They go to places you've never even thought about, or possibly even knew existed inside your company. As a result of this compulsive liar, we were as close as you can get to immediate resource with the Japanese customers, without them physically coming and picking up their tools. In fact we did ultimately have the business removed, despite the liar exiting the business.

– Use any supplier as long as they accept.

Any supplier who made comments or requests in relation to a design not being feasible was encouraged to be re-sourced. Clearly the only design possible was the one the engineers came up with, albeit it could not be manufactured consistently, and the tolerancing meant it would need to be produced in a clean room, used to make the components for the space shuttles in. I think NASA was actually one of our suppliers, or was it SANA, the Chinese were never the best at copying…..

Believe it or not there are lots of copy goods markets around (a piece of advice: whatever the price they offer, move the decimal place one place to the left). One time I was looking at football shirts. There was one for Liverpool football club. Their badge emblem says, "You'll Never Walk Alone". The Chinese version is, "You'll Never Wall Alone". Close……..

One comment on the overall question of copying and something to be conscious of. No matter what you have patented it will ultimately appear in China as a copy (the government says it is clamping down on copying. This is not very likely to happen as the industry employs so many people). There are various points in relation to this. Some of the smarter western companies getting Chinese companies to manufacture their products, deliberately design in a fault so when the parts arrive in the west they fix the fault and the product works. The copies from the Chinese will never work and they will never figure out why. There was a case in 2007 where a locally "designed" and build vehicle was actually marketed as "just like the BMW X5". In case you don't know the vehicle question was called the CEO. BMW sued and lost the case. You have been warned

One of our products originally made in the UK, and subsequently transferred to Germany, was actually copied by one of our Chinese facilities. Yes, internally they stole the design and copied it. They even copied in the insert in the die casting tool that said 'Made in England'…

A number of years before the sale of the business some UK guys went to China to find 'cheap' alternatives for a range of screw machine parts. With suitcases loaded with samples they set off for a month's adventure east. On returning they claimed victory, as if they had conquered a new world as modern day crusaders. All their samples were gone and suppliers would be submitting the first samples as quick as 'the slow boat from China' arrived in port. Duly the samples arrived and the intrepid adventurers went to work to build the products and show how easy it was to reduce the part cost of the products being made by 50%...... A day went by, which turned into a week, a week turned into a month and after six months they finally admitted that it wasn't working. Why? Well there were catalogues of reasons including:

1) They had no prints for the parts they were asking the suppliers to make.
2) The suppliers had been copying samples that were dimensionally wrong and the samples they were producing were even more inaccurate.
3) The "suppliers" they had gone to were in fact trading companies (back to the Mr Fixers).
4) The Fixers had shown the intrepid adventurers a company that looked like it could make parts, but as soon as they had left, the 'supplier' had gone to the guy down the road who clearly had no concept of what process, quality or automotive requirements were and had one 1899 lathe... Or was that the model number and in fact his was one of the lathes from 1300 BC.....not sure, in his front room? I have seen many such companies and machines and frequently got confused between Mandarin and ancient Egyptian hieroglyphics.

There is a lesson in there somewhere, however the number of companies to this day who still insist on looking to get their core technology done in China to take advantage of the 'cheap labour' is astonishing. Really all they are doing is leaving themselves open for their reputation to be destroyed and their business to suffer dramatically or even fail.

One note for anyone reading this and believing that China is still a country of low cost labour. Please think again. The days of going to China for this reason were starting to diminish in the middle of the noughties (the name occasionally given to the decade from 2000). Today the labour rate in Shanghai is equal to or even slightly higher than it is in Mexico. Many of the companies that follow cheap labour, have long since left China and moved on to other growing south east Asia economies such as Vietnam, Burma and Bangladesh.

– There was often no capability of making a decision.

"It's on the drawing, so even if the tolerances cannot be met with a specific process, just push the supplier". Again this point goes back to the overall culture of basically being told what to do. Asking a Chinese person to make a decision on something or to have an opinion on something is only likely from the ones who have been educated outside the country… and they today are the ones who will be driving the Lamborghinis, Porsches and Rolls Royce's. Incidentally, in 2008 I was told that more Ferraris were sold in China than in the rest of the world combined. During my time there I would say the average age of the people driving those cars were in their mid to late 20s. How did they get the money to afford them….? Hopefully by now you will have a better picture.

– Design reviews were poorly attended and presented.

The challenges in communication have been well documented, however attendance is another area that attracted huge concern. Attendance at meetings fell into two categories. The first one being the individuals who wanted to be seen to be attending meetings. Generally they did nothing and thought by being seen and at such meetings they were important. The other category is the people who should have been there, but did not want to attend. I mentioned earlier that the Chinese do not feel guilt, only embarrassment, and being embarrassed in a meeting was pretty serious for them. One of the worst swearwords in China is 'gang du', which literally translates to 'stupid'. To most in the West it would hardly draw a turn of the head, in China it's completely the opposite.

One other point of note on the communication side, or rather lack of it, comes from the fact that – fortunately for me – the global business language is English. To that extent I admit my failings in never mastering another language proficiently. The expectation that native English-speaking people have is that a person who is speaking English as a second or third language fully understands what you are saying and the meaning. Here are three examples of what I mean about this:

Many years ago I was working in the US in Wichita, Kansas. My boss at the time was an "Englishman" who originally came from Essex. He'd been living in the USA for 12 years and had become now an American citizen. Despite this he'd never lost his Essex accent, nor his use of slang. Ten minutes into a specific meeting a native American colleague sitting next to me, nudged me and said, "What is he talking about?"

Then, seven years ago whilst working in France, a Human Resources Manager of a particular facility and I were having a conversation on work wear. During the conversation he asked, "Where are you from?" Looking a bit confused I asked the question, "Why?" He said, "Clearly you are not from the UK as I can understand you." The penny really dropped for me subconsciously many years before I had changed the way I was communicating with people in business circumstances.

The last example I have should really hit home. Whilst working at the Shanghai facility, from time to time I would sit in on the English language lessons some 30 or so of the employees were having in the evening after work. During this one particular lesson the teacher was getting the class to spell and pronounce the word 'obamulate'. I put my hand up and asked the teacher a very simple question. "Please Miss what do you think this means?" She actually gave a pretty good answer. I said, "It's a very interesting word, but I believe that 99% of the UK population wouldn't know if you were swearing at them, asking a question or something else." She looked a little quizzical so I carried on. "The most important thing about communication, in any language, is that you can be understood. Anyone can speak words in English, but unless you put them in the right order it's just a meaningless jumble of words. The most important thing for people in this room is that they can get a message across to whoever they need to, and that they can understand that the person has understood that request. Using words that only 1% of the UK population can understand will never achieve this goal." When I explained that the word meant to walk around or to wander, the light bulbs came on in the class. The point is no matter whom you are communicating with, remember just because they come across as speaking your natural language they will rarely understand the peculiarities of a different dialect, slang or any other form of complex words. The net effect is they won't get the message and will walk out of the meeting with at best a confused understanding of what needs to be done, or worse still they will head back to the far flung parts of the business world with no intention of implementing your significantly important change. It's great to sound highly intelligent, I guess, but it's even more important that everyone can understand what the goals and objectives are, and that they go away with a common understanding.

Remember when you are speaking at 1,000 words a second (as you might well do to a native speaker of your mother tongue), with the local dialects and slang, the person smiling at you across the table will be getting one word in every ten, if they are lucky.

– Capability of generating drawings locally was poor. European faxed drawings photocopied onto a local header with hand written comments in Mandarin were the norm.

The lack of structure in the engineering department was incredible. There were cabinet files of drawings and they were accessible to literally anyone. Many had just gone missing or were of such poor quality they could not be read or worked to. I genuinely believe they had given up trying to sort the files some years previously, due simply to the sheer mass of prints and what it would have taken to get under control.

– There was no intelligence in the part numbering system.

Many companies associate certain part number sequences with a specific product. For example part numbers starting **PL123** XXXXX could signify it was a plastic injection moulding of some sort. The numbers thereafter could be used to define the type of component it was, resin type etc. This is very helpful for companies that don't have correctly implemented or followed ERP systems. In essence it makes it a little more straightforward for people to know, or to find information out. When you have a truly centralised, fully functional ERP system there are many other fields that can help to define what the component is. It's very simple thereafter to interrogate the system to find all the plastic components purchased etc. The issue at the Shanghai facility was they didn't use the ERP system and the part numbers were not intelligent. Simply put it was like looking for a needle in a haystack. Due to the lack of discipline in this area it allowed the proliferation of part numbers which allowed the continuation of the Engineering teams to reinvent the wheel

– Do Product Verification (PV) and Design Verification (DV) testing and start up with different suppliers.

– Note: - Design verification test (DVT) is an intensive testing program which is performed to deliver objective, comprehensive testing verifying all product specifications, interface standards, OEM requirements, and diagnostic commands. It consists of a number of pretty far reaching areas of testing, including:

Functional testing (including usability)
Performance testing
Climatic testing
Reliability testing
Environmental test
Mechanical test
Compliance and regulatory testing
Safety certification

So back to our Shanghai operation...... 'No one knows' what was used during the DV and PV tests. There was a specific programme where a product was failing during tests with the customer prior to start of production. The culprit supplier was identified and hauled in to be abused in public regarding their bad product. They were asked what they were doing about fixing it. The supplier, who had travelled three hours to get to the facility for their dressing down, was shown the test room and the on-going test. After five minutes of looking and looking around the room the representative from the supplier said, "I'm sorry but this is not my product." The Engineering Manager said, "Of course it's your material." The representative then walked over to a shelf and pulled an unopened package from it, saying, "This is my material." You could have heard a pin drop specifically as the Engineering Manager, to get himself off the hook, had invited the western President and western Asia Purchasing Director to the meeting. The Asia Purchasing Director, trying to suppress a smile asked "So whose material is it we are actually testing?" The meeting ended abruptly and the poor supplier had to make his three hour return journey, still no further forwards in getting their actual material tested and validated, which happened to be the one that should have been on the test rig!

– There was a lack of wanting to address issues, along with a lack of ability.

There was a specific product after it was manufactured needed to have a plastic coating extruded over it. The drawing of the part actually called this up as the finished part number and this was what was ordered from the suppliers. The challenge was that ever since the product had been introduced and first purchased it had always been supplied without the extruded plastic covering as none of the suppliers had the capability to do this. The inter-company supplier making the base product had been requesting, since before they started to produce it, a drawing which showed the product without this coating. They even went to the lengths of creating their own drawing and trying unsuccessfully to get the engineering department at the Shanghai facility to use this drawing. You might say, so what's the issue? Well two pretty fundamental ones really. Firstly it turned out to be a pretty serious non-compliance to the TS auditor who happened to pick up on it, and secondly the bill of material was incorrect. The net result was the Shanghai facility was consuming $120,000 of a single grade of resin per annum it didn't know about, which directly impacted profitability and to a constant ability to run out of the resin.....as there was no demand for it.

– Customer support on new programmes was problematic.

In 2008 there was a specific programme where we were badly late with a major European OEM in supplying samples. In total five samples were needed to be with the customer on Monday morning. I was made aware of the situation at 23:30 on the Friday night before. Making a few calls I was able to get the relevant personnel into the facility at 08:00 the following morning. The bottom line was we needed to organise a hand carry of the samples to the customer's premises by 09:00 Monday morning. The root cause of why we were in the position could be a separate book in its own right. However we simply were in this position and urgent action was needed. Samples needed to be built and made available for collection by the courier to be on a flight at 17:00 that day. The local Chinese General Manager, the Quality Manager and I headed to the prototype shop to ensure the product was being built.

The only guy in there was reluctant to build them, as he was also missing some components. So a few more calls later the Purchasing Manager arrived and the missing part suppliers were woken up and given the good news. Time was ticking by. By 16:30 the parts were being put into the packaging when the General Manager and the Quality Manager stated they would refuse to allow the shipment to go ahead. I had been working on getting the connections in place and pulling loads of favours from multiple people. Why would they not allow the consignment to be released? The cost was $15,000 and they had not tested the parts. At this point I calmly advised them the shipment was going, I was overriding their authority and they ought to consider such statements when they had knowingly shipped non-conforming product to customers on a number of occasions, just to keep their lines running knowing there would be recalls at a later stage. The consignment went, arrived in time and the whole of the management team in Europe let out a collective breath. As a final note on this the product actually passed the customers tests! Definitely more luck than judgement.

– Tooling was ordered at one supplier, then trimmed and finished by another.

The local purchasing department wanted to give it to another supplier with no experience because the supplier said they could do it! Where do you start on a subject like this? In fact you are absolving any responsibility from the company that built the tool in the first place, so if it's wrong you might as well throw the tool away and start again. The fact that the proposed supplier had no idea how to do the modifications required. The fact that the proposed supplier didn't have the equipment to do the required modifications either. The list could go on and on. I guess the message is pretty clear, but it does happen.

I was talking to a friend recently whose company is purchasing die casting in China. He told me they'd just found out their supplier had subcontracted their tooling to another company 12 months ago without any communication, document submission, nothing. The Chinese supplier did not believe they had done anything wrong, and by the way they claim to be – and have certification to prove – they are a TS accredited company…

– Start of Production (SOP) parts needed to be ordered on a regular basis prior to PPAP submission or approval.

There was a specific programme for a local OEM where the programme was starting up in production on the Monday and on the Friday of the preceding week we had not even identified a supplier base. Technically in the automotive industry this is impossible. All I can say is, "TIC!"

– There was no engineering change system.

The company was TS registered and certified, and anyone who understands TS knows such a situation technically cannot be possible. The more I thought about the accreditation the more I wondered what specific Ferrari the auditor was driving around in.

– The Shanghai facility was put on a containment Level 2 status for design.

I do not profess to be a TS expert, yet technically it is impossible to be in this situation. A containment level status is due to a specific topic. Normally it's associated with quality issues relating to a product that has been supplied. Despite discussing time and time again with the local OEM they would not remove this containment level. Even their parent group in North America told them it was not possible. As you would expect they took absolutely no notice.

– Prior to products needing to be built internal orders were generally issued to the purchasing and operations departments without lead times.

– Whatever timing plans were submitted to the customers was done by the programme managers without any consultation to the people who were going to have to deliver on them. Rather than questioning the customer and going in with facts the approach was, "……you want it tomorrow, what time…….no problems?"

– The number of Critical Characteristics (CCs) on drawings generated internally meant we were planning for failure.

It got to a point that I was convinced our engineers had developed CC Tourette's syndrome. Making a CC of something that was technically impossible to measure became an art form that group of engineers were really trying to become world class in.

Operations

– Injection moulding tooling.

The Shanghai facility had its own moulding shop before it was moved out as part of "de-complexing" the business. It was very clear looking at the state of the tooling they had never had any preventative maintenance carried out, and the three people working around every machine se-burring parts only confirmed it. The machines were equally well maintained.

Adding to this was the storage and usage of the resin. To say it was slightly confusing would be an understatement. There were no silos that the resin was fed through directly into the machines, no it was your typical receive bags of resin and tip them into a hopper. There's nothing specifically wrong with that, to this point. Some of the resins had master batch added, for a specific colour etc. Again nothing wrong with that, and common practice around the world. Then recycled materials were used. This is basically materials that have been moulded before, but rejected for parts being out of specifications etc. There were hundreds of bags of the stuff that had been cut up ready for re-use. Again nothing specifically wrong at this point in time. However, the challenge was the recycled materials were not kept separate. The process was if it was 'plastic' it went to the recycling bags and was evenly distributed across all the new virgin materials needed. Now, again for non-technical people like, me what's the issue? Well there are lots of different types of resins for a reason. Some allow for flexibility, some are used for strength, some are used to help fire protection, some quite the opposite. The bottom line is that some customers will allow a small percentage of regrind in the products you are making. Some will not let you use any regrind. However the customers or even your internal processes are insistent that if you use regrind it's the same material as the virgin stuff and not a concoction of different materials. It's a little bit like saying here's your personal car and it runs on unleaded petrol. When you go and fill up, let's put 90% unleaded petrol and the rest we will put in diesel, methylated spirits and cow's milk. I wouldn't recommend it, but you know it's possible the car may just about still work…

Another side note this wasn't just a practice happening in the Shanghai facility. During the process we were in, to get ownership of our tooling we were actually trying to cooperate with the head snake's moulding company. We had a tooling and machine specialist from Europe working and living in China with us. The one day we were with that supplier he was helping the locals understand that each tool, in each machine with each different raw material, required a different set of parameters and settings. This is something that consistently fell on deaf ears. Quite literally all moulding machines were set up to exactly the same settings for all materials and all tools. So back to the supplier visit from that day. Whilst our expert was waiting for the results of one of the trails to be analysed, he was wandering along the row of new moulding machines. He stopped at a bag of resin feeding one of our parts. He took a handful of the resin and then back in the meeting room asked, "Why are you mixing resins in our products?" The answer came, "We aren't doing that." So he showed them the sample to which they replied, "That is not possible, we don't do that…" When we returned back out to the shop floor, someone had mysteriously reported a fault on the machine and the bag of resin had disappeared. We were advised the machine was waiting a maintenance person.......

I would strongly recommend that any plastic parts you are sourcing in China are chemically analysed independently outside China. The reason is simple. You may have specified a major resin producer's material on your prints, however the likelihood of the supplier actually purchasing and receiving this material as specified is about in line with the chances of you winning the top prize in your national lottery. Remember to get the correct material they will almost certainly have to import the material. You need to add cost onto whatever you may be paying for that material in North America or Europe. It does not just become magically cheaper because it's in China. What becomes magically cheaper are the local resins being passed off as copies or equivalents of the major brand products. Remember if you are thinking about buying such parts in China:

1) Labour is a very small percentage of the cost of the product outside China. Inside China the three people per moulding machine, one watching and two de-flashing the moulded parts as the tooling had not been maintained, soon adds up.
2) The cost of resin – if you are buying the global brand product is pretty much the same rice across the globe. The only people influencing those pricings are the OEMs and I am not even sure how much influence they can bring to the table.
3) The cost of electricity does not influence the cost of the part in any significant way.
4) Freight and duty. Let's compare, if I need a part in the Czech Republic and my supplier is in, say, the Czech Republic, maybe I can order what I need and the cost of inventory will be pretty low to zero. My

transport costs are well pretty low and surprisingly there are no duty costs applicable shipping across the EU. From China the parts have to travel between 5,000 to 10,000 kilometres depending on which part of the world they are going to. It normally takes four to five weeks to get a container from China to your facility. A shipping container will cost you from $1,500 upwards for a 20 foot unit. Then on top of that you have to pay duty. You don't need to be a rocket scientist to see, it doesn't always work out the wisest decision to go down this route.

– A "goods inwards" inspection firewall installed in January 2009 shockingly revealed 100% of all deliveries were rejected in some way or other.

Working in this environment it became very difficult to be shocked, as each day would bring a new catalogue of chaos and mayhem. The good inwards inspection protocol did give that 'wow' factor though, for all the wrong reasons. Normally in a business, depending on the size of the products being purchased, you will have some sort of locked up area - maybe a largish cage - where supplier non-conforming deliveries are housed until acted on. We had to allocate a complete hall in one of the off-site warehouses to this activity. The trouble was this hall wasn't secure so parts identified as being rejected would mysteriously end up in the production parts, as some logistics guy knew where they were…. and, well, operations needed parts…. In order to improve this situation clear corrective action plans were requested from suppliers, drawings had to be changed etc. Err no, the logistics and SQE functions refused to carry on the activity as it was causing them more work and besides which Operations needed the parts… any parts…

– Decisions were often made on emotion not on facts.

There was a specific rubber part used in one of the products. For three months of the year we would have customer issues with this child part – which was being supplied directly from a company in the USA. Basically the Customer could not fit the part onto their connecting product. Strange, but every year the same thing happened at the same time. It was always an issue from December to March. Additionally the part was being supplied by a common global supplier to the company, yet nowhere else in the world were we experiencing these issues. Was it the supplier was sorting product and shipping the non-conforming product to China? Did they have a different process for the Chinese product? The answer was significantly more simple than that. However throughout the timeframe in question we had parts tested locally and by independent laboratories in North America. Significant expense was incurred for these services, not to ignore the continual rejections and charges from the Chinese OEM they were being supplied to. The answer was simply due to how we stored our child part inventories. There was no form of temperature control and in summer, when temperatures would reach 40 degrees celcius, the parts would naturally be very malleable. Guess what in winter when it dropped really cold…. you know the rest of the story. So despite the protestations of the local Chinese General Manager, desperate to blame the supplier, it was in fact his own issue and the company had paid a lot of money for nothing….again.

– Customer needs always outweighed the ability for the local management team to think in the best interests of the Shanghai facility.

I have touched on this before, however there was, across the company, an almost lemming approach as to how to deal with customers. If a customer said something it must be right. I am quite sure if our customers had said, "You have to move your factory one kilometre down the road," the building work would have started before we knew anything about it. What is strange about this is that it wasn't a dedication to supply the customer with best in class products and services, it was simply a focus so the customer would not call. Which, when you think about it, was hugely counter-productive as the customer would call even more due to the poor quality of product being shipped.

– Build to stock and not to plan.

This generated significant volumes of plastic injection mouldings, and finished goods stocks that contributed to the obsolescence. When I arrived at the facility I didn't realise you could walk around the outside of the building. The perimeter of the building was walled in and on two sides there was a lean to roof which doubled up as an additional storage location. There was so much inventory which had been produced by the mould shop it was impossible to get around. It would have been less of an issue had the inventory been something we might actually need. OK in fairness some of it was... but the vast majority was not. It definitely seemed the way they worked was more, "What resin have we got, OK we can produce this part then," whether it was required or not. Naturally this led to significant volume and more importantly values of obsolescence, not withstanding the costs of producing it in the first place. The company seemed to go through, on a quarterly basis, the process of writing off huge values on inventory. The vast majority of this obsolete material should have been disclosed and written off prior to the sale. The moulding shop was just an added negative bonus!

We eventually managed to get enough control in the mould shop to be able to move it to another of the facilities. So having very carefully agreed how we would move the machines, the local Chinese General Manager advised us he had taken care of the removal and transportation of the machines. Surely he could not get this wrong as it was pretty straightforward? Call up the company who had supplied us the machines, and get them to provide us with the name of their recommended machine mover and job done..... Err.....well, not exactly. He decided he could do it cheaper and came up with a local company he knew who was run by a 'friend'. OK so the company comes on site, and this monster fork lift truck enters the factory and eventually the first machine emerges into the daylight. The lorry to transport the machine is there and all seems to be going well. The crane is in place to lift it and then things started to go slightly askew. There are specific ways to lift a moulding machine, but lifting by attaching the ropes to the tie bars is not a recommended one. The tie bars are pretty critical to the performance of the machine and bending them under the weight of the machine really is not a cheap way to get the machine moved. The Asia Purchasing Director and I were watching this out of the office window in some amazement. The President reacted first and starts screaming at the operator to lower the machine. There then ensued a 20 minute, one way, communication from the President and lots of locals scurrying around looking for a manual as to how to lift the machine correctly. Eventually the machine was loaded correctly and the repairs to the bent tie bars could be completed somewhere else. The remaining machines were loaded under the careful watch of the President.

– Meeting actions were frequently not actioned or delivered on.

I mentioned previously about the phrase 'short cut' being patented in China. The same goes to activities relating to meetings. For our weekly management meetings the same questions invariably came up and the same answers came back. I would have to say in the majority of cases the questions could not be answered at that time because there was no data to be able to support it. The whole systemic chaos led to more and more incorrect decisions being made in the business at a local level. Had it not been for the three western expatriates at the time I am convinced the Shanghai facility would have brought the company globally to its knees. I do not say that lightly as once the snakes had exited there was nothing left to support or run the company, only situation and challenges that lead to huge drains on monies from the business and adding to that 2008 was the beginning of the last major financial crisis. Gradually over time, with the introduction of more expatriates, the plans were firmed up, the business was slowly moved, and eventually control was regained. In total it took around five years to get the business into a position where it was no longer haemorrhaging cash. At the last count there were still up to 30 expatriates living there.

– There were no controls, no accountability, no traceability and no process in the either the goods inwards inspection area or supplier parts re-work area.

On my first visit to the off-site warehouse I came across a room with a table, ten people and a load of child parts sitting on the tables. Thinking this might be an off-site sub assembly activity I asked a few questions. No this was the area where supplier's parts were re-worked before going into production. So what was happening was we were receiving the parts and the goods inwards quality people would inspect them and say, 'no'. So then the parts went next door and the workers there would basically try and get the parts to work. The majority of the work they did was to de-flash, or to remove short shot injection mouldings. They were really good as they had no documentation to work to, there were no drawings, process instructions, nothing. Once they said the parts were OK they went straight to production, even the goods inwards quality people did not re-inspect them...... Surely for this exceptional service to our suppliers there was a charge? Nope.

It was funny to see that at a time of an audit, or a customer visit, that the area never had any employees working in it and the table was always clear...

– Controlled Shipping (CS) Level 2 for production, no specifics......

I have already mentioned our CS status in the engineering section. We were – by the same local OEM – given one for production. Again this is technically impossible. You can only have such a situation for a specific quality issue relating to a supplied product. It's a shame it didn't come as a certificate from the customer, we would no doubt have proudly hung it on the wall. It had come from our customer, so it must be right...

– Overseas materials were never inspected at goods inwards' inspection.

There seemed to be this inbuilt belief with the local Chinese team that the world outside China only produces perfect parts. Supplier PPMs in the west would immediately tell you to the contrary. I believe there was a reluctance to interact with people from outside China. It would be closer to the truth to say they probably did not want to get into a disagreement with a western company. Their ability to measure things correctly was frequently called into question and their inspection equipment may not always have been up to date with the re-certification – a minor detail…

An example of maybe more of the hidden, but real, issue behind this. A number of years ago, one of the companies I was working for had a facility in Italy. There was buyer there whose English wasn't perfect, but he could absolutely communicate in English. One day he brought to my attention that a UK company were not delivering to the plan from the logistics team. So I asked him what steps he had taken. He said as soon as the logistics team had identified the risk to supply he had sent the UK company an email.

"OK," I said, "what did you do then?"

"I sent them another email," he replied.

"OK, so what did you do after that?"

"I sent them another email."

Despite the situation getting more and more critical, he basically did not have the confidence to pick up the phone and talk to the supplier. I am sure he was worried about not understanding the reply from the supplier. What he didn't realise was that the person he was sending the email to had left and the emails were not being read. One phone call and the situation was resolved. This really is an issue and culturally English-speaking nations do continue to forget this. It is vital to encourage all relevant personnel to practise and in the Shanghai facility in the logistics department I introduced an hour a day where the locals could only speak English to each other. It was a bit of fun but it really did help give them the confidence in a non-stressful environment.

So back to the Shanghai facility and any issues with materials coming from overseas were only picked up during production, and not fed back for follow up. Maybe there was a belief the issues would go away on their own......

– A number of child parts could never be inspected as there were no drawings ever generated and data sheets were not physically available in goods inwards' inspection.

However the people working in there did an amazingly good job of looking busy when Lao Wa or other managers were in the vicinity. The other questions this throws up are pretty obvious.

On the same subject we had a particular supplier who used to complain on a regular basis about his product being rejected for incorrect dimensions. So in order to bring some closure on it I invited the supplier with their inspector to our facility. We went to the goods inwards' inspection area and there we got the inspector at our facility to measure the parts as they normally would. The supplier's inspector performed the same measurements and came up with the same results. We then went over to the supplier's facility and with exactly the same parts measured them using his equipment. Both our inspector and their inspector measured the parts and got the same results. The issue was the results from the two sites were different. There was a lot of head scratching and agreement that for this supplier it would be OK to use their parts without inspection going forward! It wasn't exactly what I was expecting, however there was no understanding of what inspection protocol was at either our facility or the supplier. A simple, but real, example of a lack of effective communication also

– Testing laboratory.

For anyone who has not seen a test laboratory it always reminds me of an adult's Meccano playground. Bolted to the Meccano frames are various products you make being life cycle tested or other. Clearly the Shanghai facility had invested in the Meccano kits but had not quite understood what to do with them. There were seven people working in this area and probably this must have been one of the best jobs to have in the company. The temperature in the room was kept to a pretty consistent 75F come winter or summer and it seemed to be the perfect temperature for sleeping. The only thing missing from their office were sleeping bags. One day I went, trying to understand the status of a particular test we were running…..or supposed to be. I was in there and for 20 minutes not one of the seven people even raised an eyebrow. Fortunately I had a camera with me. Having completed photographing the evidence, I slammed, very loudly, the door behind me, making the seven people wake up with a start. The Manager of the area protested to the President that his people would never sleep in their office. Lying to the President was not a smart move and being shown the photographic evidence the Manager and his team had to exit their office…..on their way out of the company.

– The third floor.

Having been in the facility for a few months I was wandering around some of the less well known areas around the shop floor and came across a staircase that led up to a third floor. It was split into two. One half was a room with a stage big enough to sit 1,000 people. The other side was an Aladdin's treasure trove of 'stuff'. This room contained in the region of half a million dollars of finished goods inventory that 'no one' (who I my three years living there never managed to find) knew was there. Difficult to believe as it was inventory produced fairly recently, certainly in the previous six months. Digging deeper it transpired this was the inventory that was being sold to the aftermarket business illegally and against the direction of the President. How long the scam had been going on for it was impossible to tell, but there was inventory dated from three years previous. Maybe it explained how the Sales Manager was able to buy a brand new VW Passat on his pay cheque... just maybe!

Sales

− Business case submissions

These were put forward without any effective form of standard costing and frequently there was no concept on design or the resulting implications for tooling costs. In the case of one new customer, a programme was signed off with no ability for the Shanghai operation to even manufacture the product. It had been quoted based on getting one of the head snake's companies to produce it and we would literally have just re-packed and shipped. The selling price would have generated a contribution margin on this product at best case of (8%) – in other words we would have been giving monies to the Customer….along with the product. In the end I had to persuade a President from another business unit that it really was good value business for his division, and hope he could find a process to make it. Generally if a customer, for a product you have never made or supplied before, snaps your hand off with your first pricing, there is something wrong. In the end the company – not the facility - made a (12%) contribution margin. It does help if you have a business strategy for what customers and products you are going to go after. Clearly our sales colleagues clearly didn't quite understand this as a concept, and kept bringing wonderful business awards to us with ridiculously low or negative margins. So, you might ask "why would they do this?" The answer was very simple. The Sales Team were part funded (ie their bonuses) by the new business they brought it, as opposed to the "profitable" new business they brought it!! Considering how much money we were losing on the business we were supposed to be the experts at, moving outside this field did not really help....

– Commitment to customers on tooling lead times.

These were made on what the customer wanted to hear, as opposed to the actual timing that was sensible and achievable. On no occasion did a tool launch correctly in these time frames. No matter how many times we had these experiences the sales team went in for the next project and committed to the customer what they wanted to hear. Maybe the solution would have been to take the penalty costs out of their salaries!

– Customer orders were often accepted with the thinking, "This is an off the shelf product."

This specific example was a bad decision from Day one. A small producer of private transport vehicles came to us with an order we could not refuse....or more realistically did not refuse (see previous comment for probably answer). They wanted to buy 2,500 vehicle sets per annum. Now generally if you are a volume supplier of automotive parts you would laugh at the customer and tell them politely where to go. No, instead it was decided as a strategic business plan to embark on the programme. We were advised that the basis of the programme was an off-the-shelf component that represented close on to 40% of the selling price, not manufacturing cost. The customer understood this and all was going swimmingly until the second day. The second day, after signing the contract, a decision was made to change the 'off-the-shelf' product and make it bespoke. Oh and the contract with the customer gave us a fixed tooling cost. Just to produce the tooling for the bespoke product would wipe out our total contract-signed tooling budget. On the third day our engineering team then announced there would be a left hand and a right hand version of the system.... I don't want to remember the ending, however when we went into production I have vivid recollections of us attaching $50.00 to each system being supplied. It was the same Sales Manager who had been selling the aftermarket product, who had "successfully" committed us to this programme. The jury is out if it was the aftermarket or this programme or a combination of both that cemented his exit from the company. However as mentioned earlier he still left the company driving his new personal Passat....

– After accepting and starting up 'very urgent' projects customers would then delay or cancel.

Considering the growth in China during this period it seems incredible that this situation would happen.....or does it? Well maybe it's not as strange as you think. Why not get one of your suppliers to design and develop a product, and then give that design to someone else who doesn't have the overhead cost and can provide it for a lower price? Best of all they didn't even pay for the design or tooling! Surely that would never happen? OK let's not be too naïve. TIC ☺. The good news, though, was the Shanghai facility then decided it was not going to pay the suppliers.....yet more angry people threatening you!

– Customer quotations were prepared and submitted by sales without verification by other functions.

The sales department really were, up to a point, a law unto themselves. Not only did they prepare and submit the quotes, but when they had an issue with child part pricing, they turned out to have 'friends' who could make the parts for the price quoted. Wow, they were great all round guys! In one specific case we had a real issue with the pricing of some child parts. The only supplier who would agree to the pricing didn't even have the equipment to produce the parts. Even with our somewhat challenged local supply base they were considered to be a 'D' rated supplier. I am not sure what "D" rated meant, but I could certainly come up with some suitable explanations:

Do not use ever
Diabolical
Dangerous
Disastrous
Delinquent

So having refused to work with this supplier, the Sales Manager was really unhappy. He went to his customer, told them he knew of a company who could make the part for the pricing level and recommended his "friend". The next day an email came from the customer recommending this supplier. Not knowing this we duly despatched an ASQ to do a formal assessment on the company. 80% was the pass rate set for any new supplier to be on the books. 80% basically tells you the supplier has systems and shows they are following at least some of them. It basically says they should just about be able to supply your business without killing it. The audit result from our Sales Manager's friend came in at 39%. Ah, a minor gap. In essence the audit said the company could spell its own name and that was about it. Going back to the customer directly with the results of the 'imposed' company, they retracted the imposition and told us we could go wherever we wanted....but the price would not change. Everything done up to this point was based simply on price.

It is an interesting point to note that the Chinese growing middle classes don't like buying Chinese made products. There is a very clear reason. The quality levels are significantly below the levels of quality from the West. As this middle class develops they have become fed up with the poor quality and ultimately it will help to drive up improvements in the levels of quality, or at least it should. On my very first trip to China, and it didn't really sink in at the time, I was told there were two prices for the 'same' material. The Chinese price and the overseas price, each with a different quality level.

To put this into perspective the western Asia Purchasing Director decided to get his Chinese driving licence and the company gave him a well known branded vehicle, which was manufactured locally in their Shanghai facility and also in Europe. About the only thing the vehicle made in Europe and the one in China had in common was the badge on the grill looked the same. One day whilst sitting in the front passenger seat, it started raining and within a short period of time I was getting a dousing of the rain water all over me. The rain was seeping through the sun visor and providing a very un-refreshing and continuous stream of misery. The journey from the factory to the apartments was only 30 minutes, however by the time we got back it looked like I'd had a serious accident in my trousers. The vehicle dashboard, or parts of it, would literally fall out if you accelerated slightly too quickly. The driver and passenger front doors didn't quite match up to the frames well only if you slammed them hard enough would they close. The seals around the doors didn't quite do the job they were designed to. The engine blew up after 30,000 kilometres. I will stop there, however I just hope this specific OEM never,

ever decides to ship cars made in China to Europe or North America!!!

– Responsibilities between logistics, customer services and the sales departments were unclear.

Production of job specifications with roles and responsibilities was not a strength of the human resources team. In fairness they weren't helped, when you listened to the managers of the various functions as they all basically they were responsible for nothing and the actual responsibility was with one of the other functions.

– Consignment stock at the Customers was not stopped as per the demands of the President.

The same practice we were doing with our suppliers was being carried out by our customers. There was a clear instruction to stop this practice and invoice for all materials at the customer's premises. One year later we were still battling to get this implemented.

– Internal pricing was not available from previously quoted / awarded business from the days of the predecessor company.

This again all boils down to a lack of traceability. Trying to understand how pricing was determined was next to impossible. Going back to customers to ask for price increases became a necessity to quell the bleeding.

– Sales forecasts were nothing like the actual delivery situation or forecasts obtained by picking up the phone and talking to customers directly. Why should we have been surprised? There were clear cases of both extremities. Considering the level of mobile phone ownership, you might have thought the Sales team would have used these devices to actually call their customers...... Well most of the time it seemed they were used for surfing the internet and checking out those rather nice looking Passat's, shoes and other fashion accessories.....

− Customer overdues were unacceptable and resolved with the intervention of a westerner picking up the phone and talking to the customer.

On a number of occasions I personally spoke with customers and within a matter of days funds had been transferred. The customers were very open and told me that 'no one' (there he is again) had ever called from our facility and, like any good opportunist, why would you release cash if you aren't being chased for it?!

− Customer visits were rarely planned in advance and multiple customer visits occurred on the same day.

With the challenges that the facility was facing it got to the point when multiple customers would arrive without notification. Amongst the three westerners we seemed to spend a good percentage of our time sitting in front of, or at the end of a telephone talking to, customers. In many cases they were appreciative to be talking to a westerner, however I lost track of how many I times I "took one for the team". There were for sure times when I asked myself why was I doing it.

Finance

– There were no standard costs in place to effectively know if the business was making money or not.

The basis of any company is to know how much profit or loss you are making. The fundamentals of this are "know your own costs". These generally stem from understanding the standard costs of making something. Standard costs – with child parts - for example are something you generally set once per year when preparing budgets and plans for the following year. So for example, if you are paying a dollar for something, come the time of budgeting you say this is now my standard cost. If over the next 12 months the price changes you have a variance to your standard cost, which will result in you either losing money or making money depending on which way the price has moved. Pretty straightforward you would think. Well, unfortunately not. Due to the way materials were ordered and from who they were ordered, it was possible to have three or maybe more different prices available for the same parts. Either way, for standard costing to work effectively you generally have to be using an ERP system. It's for sure possible to do it manually albeit with the number of different bills of materials in a business like that, totally impractical.

Another pre-requisite is to have correct bills of materials. It's not just the child parts that need to have standards set. It's the labour, the processes and pretty much everything should have a standard to measure against. Any elements that are not there render standard costing impossible, and you are back to pure guesswork. It becomes more in line with how much money came in in the month and how much went out.

This when I first went to China was a general approach from the companies I met and initially worked with to business. I remember my first ever negotiation in China was, putting it simply, a haggle. The price remained in effect for the life of the programme, however it is pure speculation if that pricing was commercially viable to the supplier or not

– Invoice processing was done without the level of detail to be expected in Europe or the Americas.

When raising this question to a visiting western finance Director his statement was, "You have to trust your employees." OK, clearly someone who had his head stuck up his backside and experienced in the ways of the world... or not. Considering this specific Chinese facility was the only one worldwide not following the company finance standard rules it was a doubly questionable statement. Even the wholly owned facility followed the company finance rules…...

– Monies and assets were transferred from one company to another without any board of Director approval.

This may, in corporate world beliefs, be impossible to do. Unfortunately it's a lot easier than you may think. Doing something about it in China is actually a lot more complicated and not guaranteed to be a success. You could always try a personal prosecution, if your ex-employee ever sets foot again in your suing country. This is unlikely though, as the dividends gained from the transfer will certainly outweigh the risks in their eyes.

– Invoice matching process never shows up deviations

to purchase order prices.

– Pricing was keyed into the system at time of invoice receipt to ensure they matched up. Is this bad practice or corruption? You can decide. The fact it happened shows the lack of controls on the purse strings, however what do you expect when your CFO couldn't even tell you where China was, and told you just to trust the people managing the purse strings!

Here I am going to relate to a different company in a different environment, yet the same scenario. There was a question mark over the practice of a Human Resources Manager in a far flung part of this company's business empire. The individuals who had witnessed the alleged acts of corruption had reported them via the company 'confidential help line', set up for just this purpose. These calls were monitored by the global Vice President of the department, who would recommend any actions to be taken. The said Vice President was so unwilling to travel that they told the Manager who the allegations had been made against to instigate the investigation! Needless to say that company ended up with two employees fewer and almost certainly the local Manager was able to carry on whatever the alleged practices were. Who says it pays to be honest? The serious message here is how can you lead something if you have no interest or desire to be part of the solution? Having people you can trust is of paramount importance, but do not fall into the trap of trusting too much.

– Late payment of invoices resulted in a number of overseas suppliers imposing pro-forma terms as opposed to credit terms.

Whilst the process of paying local suppliers seemed to run without any controls, the payment of overseas suppliers was a separate question entirely. For sure it had consequences and it only went to hurt a bleeding business still further.

Summary

There are many more examples that could be provided in lots of different areas both inside the company and outside however the aim of this guide was to be just that. It was never, and could never be an encyclopaedia of what to do in any given situation. It has I hope however give you a flavour of the realities of life and reasons to give as much focus to this corner of the world as you would to any other.

The situation the Shanghai facility found itself in after the acquisition could never have been fully known or understood before, during or immediately after the due diligence process. You could say that was the fault of the company buying the business, and for sure there is a lot of truth in that, however I would look at this case as more of a 'perfect storm'. All the worst of possible elements came together at the same time and the net result was truly ugly. For anyone who has lived through something similar you have my sympathies. For anyone reading this and saying its fiction then I look forward to reading about the success of your next venture in China, by following the same path. The straightjackets are on order.

The deliberate hiding of information and blatant lying that has been done by certain members of the company being sold had an unfortunate adverse effect for the vast majority of professional people employed by that company. The effect of it being very few of those people in managerial positions would ever make it there. Everyone ended up being tarred with the same brush.

There are many lessons that could and should be learnt from such an experience, however daily you see or hear of companies getting into difficulty because they do not understand how to do business outside their home territory. For sure there will be and are successes out there. At the core of those successes will be people who actually understand how to adapt business to different parts of the world and the need to start with the first critical element which is your company business culture. Never forget it. It's what your reputation is built on, it stands for everything you believe in so don't throw it all away just because you hear the local Fixer saying, "ah but business works differently in China." It absolutely will if you allow it.

Never trust anything until you see it yourself. Doing business in China and trying to manage it from the West is planning for failure.

Remember joint ventures are a little bit like being half pregnant. Clearly in some countries and industries you can't have WOFEs, and if your intention is to still go ahead make sure you have very strong representation from your management to give it a chance of succeeding. Otherwise it will be you who will probably be writing the next *Lessons Learnt* book.

I started this book advising that China is a country you will either love or hate, and I still stand by that. Despite the brutal and ugly times I experienced, it is still a phenomenal country with an incredible culture, history and people. I am eternally grateful to have met some wonderful people whilst working and living in China. Remember everywhere you go in the world there is good, bad and ugly. In every country there is corruption on varying scales, or have we already forgotten what started the last global crisis, or politicians in the UK claiming for expenses they never incurred? The examples could go on and on.

As a final comment, doing business anywhere in the world you are not familiar with is fraught with challenges and difficulties and how you approach those situations is what is fundamentally important.

CPSIA information can be obtained at www.ICGtesting.com
Printed in the USA
LVOW13s1354180614

390598LV00005B/360/P